Dietary
and Lif
Therap cs to
Adrenal Fatigue Syndrome

Your Personal Recovery Toolbox

Michael Lam, M.D., M.P.H.

Dorine Lam, R.D., M.S., M.P.H.

Dietary and Lifestyle Therapeutics to Adrenal Fatigue Syndrome:
Your Personal Recovery Toolbox
by Michael Lam, M.D., M.P.H. and Dorine Lam, R.D., M.S., M.P.H.

Published in the United States by:

Adrenal Institute Press, Loma Linda, CA 92354
www.AdrenalInstitute.org

Cover and Interior Design: Nick Zelinger, NZ Graphics
Editing: John Maling (Editing By John), Virginia McCullough
Book Shepherding: Judith Briles

The authors of this book do not dispense medical advice or prescribe the use of any technique or natural compounds as forms of prevention and treatment for physical, emotional, or medical programs without the advice of a physician, either directly or indirectly. The intent of the authors is only to offer information of a general nature to help you in your quest for well-being. This book is not meant to replace the advice and treatments prescribed by your healthcare provider. It is not meant to encourage treatment of any illness by the layman. In the event you use any of the information in this book for yourself, which is your right, you assume risk, and the authors and the publishers assume no responsibilities for your actions. If you are under a physician's care for any condition, he or she can advise you about information described in this book. The authors or publisher shall have neither liability for nor responsibility to any person or entity with respect to any loss, damage, injury caused or alleged to be caused directly or indirectly by the information contained in this book.

Any trademarks, service marks, product names, or named features are assumed to be the property of their respective owners, and are used only for reference. There is no implied endorsement if we use one of these terms.

ISBN (paperback): 978-1-937930-09-7
ISBN (ebook): 978-1-937930-10-3
Library of Congress Control Number: 2012936520

Dietary and Lifestyle Therapeutics to Adrenal Fatigue Syndrome: Your Personal Recovery Toolbox / Michael Lam, Dorine Lam. First edition, 2012; Includes Index

10 9 8 7 6 5 4 3 2 1

1. Health 2. Adrenal glands—Disease. 3. Fatigue 4. Stress (Physiology) 5. Neuroendocrine

First Edition

Printed in the United States of America

Contents

Author's Note

When Adrenal Fatigue Syndrome has entered your life, especially in the advanced stages, the lifestyle as you knew it is significantly impaired. In a word, you are exhausted and the simple act of sitting down at the table with family to enjoy an evening meal becomes an almost impossible feat.

You want your life back.

Diet, sleep, relationships, and exercise are important components in any Adrenal Fatigue Syndrome recovery program. To be effective, each component must be personalized to one's unique inborn constitution. *Dietary and Lifestyle Approaches to Adrenal Fatigue Syndrome: Your Personal Toolbo*x will go in depth into each of these areas and is certain to aid in your recovery.

Dr. Lam

Note: This book is part of Dr. Lam's Adrenal Recovery Series™ and all information can be found in *Adrenal Fatigue Syndrome: Reclaim Your Energy and Vitality with Clinically Proven Natural Programs.*

Introduction

Fatigue and lethargy are two of the most common complaints doctors hear from their adult patients, both of which are symptoms of a silent epidemic condition known as Adrenal Fatigue Syndrome (AFS). This condition is as old as humankind, but its incidence has skyrocketed as our society and our lifestyles have become increasingly complex and high-pressured.

From a sufferer's point of view, Adrenal Fatigue Syndrome is confusing and frustrating. We can see the everyday consequences of Adrenal Fatigue Syndrome in the following statements:

- I'm tired all the time—I manage to keep going on my job, but I drink coffee every few hours to get through
- I used to merely gripe and complain about feeling tired, but now the fatigue is so overwhelming and debilitating, I'm underperforming on my job.
- I'm anxious and fearful much of the time.
- I seem to catch every cold or flu that comes around.
- My joints ache, and my doctor said I probably have arthritis, even though I just turned 40.
- I'm depressed and can't think straight—I feel like I walk around with brain fog.
- I've tried every diet in the book, but I can't lose weight.
- I wake up at 3:00 AM and toss and turn for hours and cannot fall asleep again.
- I used to have great energy, but now a short walk wears me out.

These statements personalize some of the typical—and persistent—signs and symptoms of Adrenal Fatigue Syndrome. You might have described these same things to your doctor, or you may have noted these changes in your health or know someone who has these complaints, but you don't know what to make of them. If you're over age forty-five or fifty, you might even be told to attribute your symptoms to "normal" aging!

Below, you'll find an expanded list of the signs and symptoms of Adrenal Fatigue Syndrome. Not surprisingly, many of these symptoms are also related to other conditions, and they match the statements listed above:

- Often feels tired between 9:00 and 10:00 PM, but resists going to bed
- Difficulty getting out of bed in the morning
- Cravings for salty, fatty, and high protein food such as meat and cheese
- For women, increased symptoms of PMS and irregular menstrual bleeding, with days of heavy flow that stops (or nearly stops) on day 4, only to resume on days 5 or 6 of the menstrual cycle
- Pain in the upper back or neck with no apparent reason
- Tendency to feel better on vacation and when stress is relieved
- Food and or inhalant (air borne) allergies
- Dry and thin skin
- Hypoglycemia but blood sugar is normal
- Low body temperature despite thyroid medication

- Heart palpitations when heart is normal
- Unexplained hair loss
- Recurrent miscarriages in the first trimester
- Low blood pressure, dizziness, and vertigo

As you can see, Adrenal Fatigue Syndrome has a broad spectrum of symptoms, many of which seem nonspecific, and, therefore, are often reframed as psychological in origin, such as anxiety or depression. Sometimes patients are told that these symptoms are "nothing that some rest won't cure." However, it is clear that Adrenal Fatigue Syndrome is not that simple. Research shows that AFS at its core represents the body's neuroendocrine stress response when under threat.

Do not confuse AFS with Addison's disease.

Addison's disease is often caused by an autoimmune dysfunction, whereas stress and a host of other factors are the primary culprits of Adrenal Fatigue Syndrome. The symptoms of Addison's disease include low energy, joint and abdominal pain, weight loss, diarrhea, fever, and electrolyte imbalances. Some AFS sufferers report these symptoms too, but they are usually much less intense.

Both lead to low cortisol output in the adrenal glands, though those with AFS can be symptomatic despite the fact that laboratory tests are usually normal. Currently, conventional medicine recognizes only Addison's disease as a legitimate disease of low adrenal function. If, for example, you ask your doctor if your symptoms could point to Adrenal Fatigue Syndrome, you may learn that he or she has not heard of AFS or may deny its existence.

Adrenal Fatigue Syndrome (AFS) consists of four broad and overlapping clinical stages, from mild to severe. Stages 1 (Alarm

Reaction) and 2 (Resistance Response) are generally mild. Some fatigue is present, but not debilitating. Few are alerted and seek professional help. By the time Stage 3 (Adrenal Exhaustion) arrives, most have seen their physician for lack of energy and are usually told all is well after an extensive workup. Fatigue in Stage 4 (Adrenal Failure) is severe and most sufferers are bedridden.

Chapter 1

A Healing Diet for Adrenal Fatigue Syndrome

A poor diet, or one that is incompatible with individual needs, is a key and leading cause of Adrenal Fatigue Syndrome. Without a diet that is biochemically and metabolically compatible with the needs of a damaged adrenal gland, it's simply not possible to achieve complete recovery.

> **Note: The dietary guidelines mentioned in this chapter are designed for those in Stage 3 of Adrenal Fatigue Syndrome, a point at which adopting a diet that promotes healing is especially important. However, many of these guidelines would benefit others in earlier stages of AFS, along with individuals who would like to build their health and *prevent* AFS.**

Glucose/Sugar

Glucose is a simple sugar found in food. It is an essential nutrient that provides energy for the proper functioning of the body's cells. After meals, food is digested in the stomach and is broken down into glucose and other nutrients. The glucose is absorbed by the intestinal cells and carried by the bloodstream to cells throughout the body. However, glucose cannot enter the cells alone. It needs assistance from insulin in order to penetrate the cell walls. Insulin therefore acts as a regulator of glucose transport and metabolism in the body.

The Hunger Hormone

Insulin is also referred to as the *hunger hormone.* As the blood sugar level increases after a meal, the corresponding insulin level rises. For energy, glucose is transported from the blood into the cell. As energy is produced by the cell, the blood glucose level is slowly lowered, and the insulin released from the pancreas is turned off. As energy continues to be generated, the blood sugar level continues to drop. When blood sugar drops below a certain level, we feel hunger, which often develops a few hours after a meal. This drop in blood sugar triggers the adrenals to make more cortisol. The cortisol increases the blood sugar by converting protein and fat into its component parts. With this, the blood sugar rises to provide a continuous supply of energy to use between meals. Cortisol, therefore, works hand-in-hand with insulin to provide a steady blood sugar level twenty-four hours a day and keeps blood glucose levels in a tightly controlled range.

Carbohydrates, Proteins, and Fats

For Adrenal Fatigue Syndrome sufferers, it's especially important to balance the macronutrients: protein, fat, and carbohydrates. Those with AFS have an immediate need for sugar (glucose) when hunger strikes. However, to have sustained energy until the next mealtime they also need good protein as well as good fat. Therefore, the snack choice should resemble the components of regular meals.

Eating Schedule

It's important for those with AFS to commit to a program of regular meals. Hunger is a complicated issue, and no two people have the same sensations that signal when it's the right time to eat or abstain. For example, some of us have no appetite when our cortisol levels peak from 6:00-8:00 AM, and we may skip breakfast because we're not hungry. However, our bodies need fuel (glucose) to run on, the body's energy requirements don't change during this period of early morning. Even a small snack is better than nothing at all and will provide needed energy, even if you have no urge to eat.

If your blood sugar is low, the body instructs the adrenals to secrete cortisol because it activates *gluconeogenesis* (the synthesis of glucose from non-carbohydrate molecules, i.e., amino acids or fatty acids) to increase blood sugar levels, thereby allowing the body to function. This is why it's important to eat a healthy breakfast soon after waking and not later than 10:00 AM. An adequate breakfast prevents the body from having to play catch-up for the rest of the day.

Ideally, you'll eat lunch between 12:15 and 12:45 PM. Sometimes we need a nutritious snack between 2:30 and 3:00 PM in order to sustain our bodies through the dip in cortisol levels that occurs between 3:00 and 4:00 PM. Then, the evening meal follows, ideally between 6:00 and 7:00 PM. In other words, every 3-4 hours, you should eat something healthy that includes some fat and protein.

All meals, which needn't be large, are best planned using low-glycemic index foods. (See Appendix B for a complete list.) It is important to avoid consuming high-glycemic index foods such as refined flour and high-sugar baked goods, fruit, and other desserts, especially by themselves. These sugary, high-carbohydrate snacks cause the blood sugar to rise, triggering a corresponding increase in insulin output. Then, over time, insulin secretion becomes dysfunctional, resulting in a hypoglycemic state during the day and in the middle of the night, which manifests in symptoms such as anxiety, jitteriness, dizziness, nightmares, and night sweats. When this occurs, the body must activate the adrenals to put out more cortisol in order to raise the blood sugar back to its normal level. If this situation continues year after year, we eventually put an excessive burden onto the already fatigued adrenal gland.

The Primary Adrenal Fatigue Syndrome Diet

The primary diet for AFS is designed for those in Stage 3. However, as you can see, some of the guidelines are beneficial for most people, including those with sensitive blood sugar issues, allergies, or those who would like to adopt an anti-aging diet.

For optimal AFS recovery, design your diet to be high in raw food and low on the glycemic index (GI). Consider the following guidelines:

- Start each morning with a full glass of water and half a teaspoon to one teaspoon of sea salt as tolerated.
- Provided blood pressure is normal, sprinkle sea salt liberally on food to taste. (Foods high in potassium, such as bananas and dried figs, raisins, and dates can make the adrenals worse, so those in Stage 3 should avoid them.)

- Eat frequently—five to six small meals instead of three large ones, which means eating every 3-4 hours.
- Avoid fruit juices of all kinds.
- Avoid eating whole fruits alone, especially melons, which are high on the glycemic index, because sugar spikes soon after ingestion. It is best to eat fruits before a meal or that contain some protein.
- *Include in moderation:* organically grown fruits such as papayas, mangos, apples, grapes, berries, and cherries.
- Choose good quality protein from meat, fish, poultry, and eggs; these foods provide a steady source of energy between meals.
- Combine generous protein and fat at every meal and snack to maintain your energy supplies.
- If you have difficulty falling asleep, eat some protein and fat, such as nuts, turkey, chicken or eggs before retiring.
- If you tend to wake up in the middle of the night, eat a small healthy snack high in protein and fat, such as cottage cheese or nuts before going back to sleep.
- Avoid foods that stimulate the body, such as caffeinated coffee, caffeinated soft drinks, green tea and regular tea.
- Avoid foods that may increase inflammation in the body, such as wheat and dairy.
- If you have OAT axis imbalance, avoid foods that can cause hormonal imbalance such as unfermented soy like tofu and cruciferous vegetables.

- Avoid foods that stress the liver, such as alcohol.
- Avoid foods that cause more stress on the body, such as fried foods, refined foods, and highly processed foods.
- If you can find it, use raw (non-pasteurized) dairy. It's very nutritious. This is an exception to the guideline above that advises avoiding dairy. Further, goat milk is better than cow's milk for human consumption. Otherwise, avoid dairy as much as possible. The protein casein and the fats found in milk are chemically changed during the high heat of pasteurization, which creates more stress and promotes inflammation.
- Drink two cups of chicken broth (discussed next chapter) daily to help prevent the body from further breakdown of collagen and muscle—the body itself. Chicken broth provides gentle nutrients, easily absorbed by the catabolic body, thereby preventing further breakdown of collagen and muscle.
- To help the body clear the toxins, it is important to drink 8-10 cups of water daily. Add lemon slices or a splash of lemon juice to drinking water to gently improve liver function.
- Avoid fruits in the morning to prevent overloading the body with potassium and sugar.

If You Have Digestive Concerns

Those with digestive issues should take digestive enzymes and probiotics before each meal. In addition, it's also important to select the proper food combination at each meal to prevent bloating and gas. Correct food combinations help to improve digestion, meaning the use and assimilation of the nutrients in the diet. Here are some guidelines:

- Avoid eating fruits and vegetables in the same meal.
- Avoid eating starch and protein in the same meal.
- Vegetables and meat, or, vegetables and starch, can be eaten in the same meal.
- Many AFS sufferers have a lower level of hydrochloric acid (HCI), which is necessary to break down proteins. Symptoms of low-HCI include gas, bloating, and heaviness in the stomach after eating a meal containing protein. In such case, it's beneficial to take digestive en zymes, probiotics (acidophilus and other intestinal flora), as well as taking HCl replacements.
- If you feel worse after consuming certain foods, realize that this is the body's way of telling you that you are on the wrong track.

If You Have Acid Reflux

- Do not drink liquid during your meal. It's best to drink liquid between meals.
- Eat small meals—this guideline is especially important for those with acid reflux.
- Take digestive enzymes and hydrochloric acid before meals.
- Do not lay flat immediately after a meal.
- Take probiotics.

If You Have Food Sensitivities

Keeping a food journal is an effective and important way to identify foods that you are sensitive to. Once you have identified the food, avoid it. As your adrenals become stronger, you likely will find your food sensitivities decreasing. It is best to eat these foods only once every 7 days. For example, if you eat an allergenic food today, then don't eat the same food again for 4-5 days. It takes a food 4-5 days to clear out of your system; some foods take up to 7 days to clear.

A Word to Vegetarians

Vegetarians with AFS face a bigger challenge than others because of the nature of protein. Animal proteins contain complete proteins, meaning they provide *essential amino acids.* To clarify, 20 amino acids form the building blocks of the body's proteins, including muscles, tendons, organs, glands, nails, and hair. Our cells depend on proteins for growth, repair, and maintenance. *Essential* amino acids are so named because they must be obtained from the diet in the form of complete proteins, whereas the body manufactures nonessential amino acids from other sources that provide some but not all amino acids.

The body can produce 10 of the 20 amino acids, and we must supply the others through the food we eat. If we're missing the amino acids we can't produce, the body's proteins, such as muscle, begins to degrade. The body stores fat and starch, but it doesn't store excess amino acids, which is why the body demands protein every day.

Vegetarians have a challenge to obtain the *complete* proteins (containing all the essential fatty acids). The first step involves becoming educated about *food combining.* Animal protein, i.e., meat, dairy, eggs, poultry, and fish are complete proteins because they contain sufficient levels of all essential amino acids. Very few plant sources, one being soybeans, contain all the essential amino acids, which is why vegetarians need to be especially careful to ingest proteins that when combined form a complete protein. Lacto-ovo vegetarians are those who include dairy foods and eggs in their diet, and these foods provide complete proteins. Vegans eat plant foods only.

What is a Complementary Protein?

We derive plant proteins, which provide one or more essential amino acids, from foods such as beans, nuts, seeds, legumes, and soy products. For example, rice contains lysine, but beans tend to be low in that amino acid. However, when ingested together, these two foods make up a complete protein with adequate levels of the essential amino acids. In other words, these proteins complement each other. Vegetarians must plan their meals to make sure that the missing amino acids in one food are provided by another food eaten during the rest of the day.

We do not recommend relying solely on dairy products and eggs for complete proteins. Vegetarians and others should eat whole grains on a 4-5 day rotational basis. In other words, avoid eating the same grains day after day, but instead, vary them through rotation.

You will find complementary proteins in ethnic cuisines—and in some "humble" everyday foods that are staples in the west, including the Southern hemisphere. Traditional Middle Eastern and Asian cuisine also contain complementary proteins. However, few cultures across the globe rely 100 percent on plant foods to meet protein needs. Here are some dishes that contain complementary proteins:

- Beans with corn tortillas
- Tofu* with rice

- Almond butter on wheat/rye bread*
- Hummus with pita bread
- Chickpeas and other beans combined with rice

*Wheat and many soy foods are not recommended for the AFS diet. However, you can add miso or tempeh to your diet. (See Chapter 25, *Food and Chemical Sensitivities*, for more about wheat.)

Soy and OAT Axis Imbalance

If you are a woman with advanced Adrenal Fatigue Syndrome, it's likely you have developed some OAT axis imbalance. Soy acts like estrogen in your body, which adds to issues of estrogen dominance. Soy also affects the *goitrogens* (substances that suppress thyroid function) in the thyroid glands.

Ample evidence exists that the isoflavones found in soy products, including genistein, are toxic to the body. For example, isoflavones inhibit thyroid peroxidase, which makes T3 and T4. In other words, these elements of soy products interfere with the production of vital components of the thyroid hormone.

Unfermented soy products, such as tofu and infant soy formula, contain:

- Allergens
- Enzyme inhibitors
- Hormone modifiers
- Mineral blockers
- Iodine blockers that interfere with thyroid function

Since the late 1950s, researchers have identified soy as a *phytoestrogen*, meaning a plant-based element with an estrogenic effect of about 1/500 the potency of the body's naturally circulating estrogen. Soy acts as a competitive inhibitor of estrogen at the cellular estrogen receptor site, reducing the effect of estrogen in your body. At the same time, over consuming soy can overwhelm many of the body's cells and may overload them.

How much is too much? This varies depending on age. For adults, just 30 mg of soy isoflavones per day is the amount found to have a negative impact on thyroid function. We can easily get 30 mg of soy from just 5-8 ounces of soy milk or 1.5 ounces of miso. Interestingly, while miso has a phytoestrogenic effect, it does not have the enzyme inhibitory effect because it is fermented. Other fermented soy products include soy sauce and tempeh.

What the AFS Diet Looks Like

As a general guideline, your daily diet should include:

- 30-40 percent above-the-ground vegetables (i.e., green leafy vegetables, winter and summer squash, tomatoes, green beans, celery, salad greens, and so forth). Broccoli, cauliflower, and cabbages are included, but we recommend reducing the amounts of these vegetables to no more than twice a week due to their estrogenic properties. About 50 percent of the daily vegetables should be consumed raw if possible provided they are tolerated.

Note: Vegetables such as carrots and turnips are root vegetables and grow below the ground. Consuming root vegetables raw is okay, because you can't consume too

much of them. It is okay to eat cooked sweet potatoes, turnips, carrots, and beets in smaller quantities, i.e., half a cup a day.

- 10-20 percent grains
- 10-20 percent beans and legumes.
- 20-30 percent animal foods, i.e., *organic* hormone- and antibiotic-free meats and poultry, such as turkey and chicken, as long as these products. Deep sea, mercury free fish (i.e., wild caught salmon and shrimp and some tuna caught in Canadian and U.S. waters) are allowed, too. Seafood must be purchased carefully because of the continuing issue of mercury and other substances polluting oceans and fresh water and adversely affecting living organisms.
- 20-30 percent good fats, i.e. nuts and seeds, extra virgin olive oil, coconut oil, grape seed oil, rice bran oil, avocado, flax seed, walnut oil. Purchase high quality, cold pressed oils.
- 10-15 percent whole fruits (except banana, fruits in the melon family,and dried fruits) taken with some protein.

Note: You'll notice that the minimum percentages add up to 100 percent. The ranges however, are approximations and will vary day-to-day. Perhaps one day will include slightly more fat than fruit, for example. We recognize that the exact plan varies from person-to-person, and no one-size-fits-all approach exists. We customize

dietary plans for those who seek our help in order to match the body's caloric and nutritional requirements according to the body's ability to assimilate. Those who are in advanced AFS, especially those in Stage 3C and 3D, often have poor assimilation and cannot tolerate most of the above general recommendations.

Tilting Toward Raw Foods

About 50-60 percent of the diet should consist of raw food, which means it's important to include 6-8 servings of a wide variety of vegetables each day. Vegetables high in sodium, and therefore recommended for AFS sufferers, include kelp, black olives, red hot peppers, spinach, zucchini, celery, and Swiss chard.

The easiest way to consume these vegetables involves introducing at least three types of different colored vegetables at your meals. For example, toss a salad of green and red leaf lettuce, spinach, red or yellow bell peppers, and celery. Use broccoli, carrot, cauliflower, zucchini, and red and green cabbages and/or bell peppers in other salads or in a vegetable stir fry. Add nutrients to meals with steamed or sautéed kale, Swiss chard, and other green leafy vegetables. You can add extra flavor to salads by adding a variety of chopped herbs such as basil, mint, parsley, cilantro, and green onions.

Multicolored vegetables, including many vegetables listed above, provide antioxidants (which help clear toxins and protect the cell) and phytonutrients (plant-derived nutrients) that benefit the body. These vegetables can be used both cooked and raw, because some phytonutrients deliver health benefits when heated. Still, a spinach salad, for example, has health benefits, too. As good as raw food is, not everyone finds it tolerable. The more advanced the AFS, the less tolerant of raw food one can be.

Seeds and Nuts

These are critical components of the diet and are sources of some amino acids and fatty acids, which the adrenal glands need to manufacture cholesterol, a precursor to all adrenal steroid hormones. Choose fresh raw nuts and seeds that are free of rancid (spoiled) oils.

Note: Rancid oils create and/or worsen symptoms of AFS, so avoid at all cost. Rancid oils, rancid nuts and seeds smell "off." We recommend storing nuts and seeds in the refrigerator or freezer.

With the exception of peanuts, liberally include raw nuts in your diet. Excellent choices include: almonds, cashews, Brazil nuts, pecans, walnuts, hazel nuts, macadamia, chestnuts, pumpkin seeds, pine nuts, and so forth. Soak brown colored nuts at least 12 hours before eating; soak brown colored seeds 2-4 hours before eating. Soaking helps improve absorption by removing an enzyme inhibitor in the brown coating. Avoid peanuts because of the potential for allergic reaction among some people; in addition, peanuts may be contaminated with the mold aflatoxin.

Everyday Fats and Oils

The following tips are useful as you plan your meals:

- Use olive, avocado, flax seed, or walnut oil—cold pressed—for salad dressings, but not for high heat cooking. When heated, the chemical structure of beneficial oils changes and at higher temperatures will transform into trans-fats, which cause oxidative stress in the body.

- When cooking with these oils, in a stir fry, for example, use enough water to stir fry and steam the vegetables. Then add one of the above oils and seasoning after the vegetables are done cooking and you've turned off the stove burner. If you want to sauté or stir fry with oil, use grape seed or rice bran oil, which have higher boiling points.
- Butter improves the flavor of some foods—don't be afraid to use it.
- Use coconut oil and olive oil in protein smoothies to improve the number on the GI (glycemic index).

Sugar

We recommend avoiding foods high in sugar in order to avoid imbalances in blood sugar, which can lead to hypoglycemic reactions, discussed earlier in this book. Avoiding high sugar content foods also gives you evenly balanced energy levels throughout the day. Sugar is both an *overt* and *hidden* food. Avoid fruit juices, soda, and alcoholic drinks. Also, avoid ice cream and pastries, candy and cake—and on and on—foods that are obvious sources of sugar. These sweet foods are also called empty calories because they are high in calories, but low in nutrients. Hidden sources of sugar include many commercial salad dressings and sauces, including popular pasta and tomato sauces.

Decreasing sugar intake helps to improve the immune system, which in turn, helps the adrenal recovery, and reducing or eliminating the empty calories of sugar will help weight loss efforts.

Breakfast Ideas

It's true! Breakfast really is the most important meal of the day. It provides the necessary nutrients to start the day after the body has been in a fast during the night. This first meal of the day should include some protein and fats, along with some carbohydrates. Here are some suggestions:

- We agree with the old adage, *an apple a day keeps the doctor away*, so spread some almond or cashew butter (but not peanut butter) on apple slices. Or, eat an apple with a handful of nuts. Cut up fruits or berries into a bowl of wheat-free or gluten-free granola or wheat-free, whole-grain cereal, and then add whole milk yogurt.

- Be creative and make a delicious protein shake with protein powder (rice or whey, but not soy), raw hormone-free organic eggs, avocado, coconut oil, berries, and other fruits.

- Many individuals believe that consuming raw eggs is dangerous because of potential contamination with salmonella, a serious food borne bacterium. However, raw eggs are safe because salmonella exists in the eggshell, not inside the egg. If you carefully wash eggs before storing them, they are safe to use raw. Raw egg contains the best source of protein as well as un-oxidized cholesterol. It is truly one of nature's best gifts to AFS sufferers.

- You can also include soft boiled eggs and add a steamed or baked sweet potato.

- Cooked oatmeal with added ground nuts, berries or other fresh fruit, and coconut flakes is a good breakfast on a cold day.

Sample Food Plan, based on 2000 calories a day

Whole grains 10% = 200 calories = 1 slice of Ezekiel Sprouted Wheat bread, 1/2 cup of brown rice, and 1/4 cup of oatmeal, for example.

Vegetables 10% = 200 calories = 3 cups salad, 2 cups green leafy vegetables, and 2 cups mixed vegetables.

Root vegetables or starchy vegetables 10% = 200 calories = 1 cup winter squash, 1 sweet potato, 1 carrot, and potatoes in *small* quantities, such as homemade hash-brown potatoes, fingerling, or purple potatoes. Do not eat deep fried commercial and restaurant french fries or hash browns. The fats in these foods are unhealthy.

Beans or legumes 10% = 200 calories = half to one cup beans and legumes, such as black beans or lentils.

Nuts, seeds 15% = 300 calories = 1 oz nuts and seeds and 1 tbsp nut butter, for example.

Fat 15% = 300 calories = 1 tablespoon of olive oil, 0.5 tablespoon of coconut oil, and 0.5 tablespoon of butter.

Animal proteins 20% = 400 calories = 5 oz meat, chicken, fish, or eggs.

Whole fruits 10% = 200 calories = 2.5 medium whole fruits such as apple.

Adrenal Diet Do's and Don'ts

The following table summarizes and clarifies the dietary guidelines and the reasons for them.

Adrenal Fatigue Syndrome Diet by Michael Lam, MD, MPH, and Dorine Lam, RD, MS, MPH	
Goals	
1) Eat before 10:00 AM.	
2) Eat frequent, small meals: breakfast 6-8 AM, lunch 12-1 PM, dinner 6-7 PM, snacks 10 AM, 3 PM, and bedtime.	
3) Eat 10-20% whole grains, 30-40% vegetables (50% should be raw), 10-20% beans and legumes, 20-30% animal foods, 10-15% fruit, 20-30% good fats, nuts and seeds.	
Avoid	
Banana, dried figs, raisins, dates, oranges, grapefruit	High in potassium - makes Adrenal Fatigue Syndrome worse
Fruit and juice in the morning	Raise and drop blood sugar fast
Refined flour products: pasta, white rice, bread, pastry, baked goods	Drops blood sugar fast, robbed of nutrients; wheat may cause inflammation in the body

Honey, sugar, syrups, soft drinks	Drops blood sugar too fast within one hour
Coffee, tea, black tea, hot chocolate, alcohol, colas, chocolates	Caffeine stimulates the body; alcohol causes liver congestion
Avoid foods you are addicted to or allergic or sensitive to	Cause additional stress on your body
Avoid rushed and hectic meals	Creates more stress for your body
Avoid deep-frying and browning; hydrogenated oils	Trans fats increase inflamma-tion in the body
Most Beneficial	
Eat before 10 AM. supply	Replenishes waning glycogen
Eat frequent small meals Keep blood sugar and insulin balanced	Coast through low energy periods
Bedtime snack (use soaked raw nuts)	Helps to have more peaceful sleep

Combine fat, protein, and whole grains at every meal and snack	Provides a steady source of energy over a longer period of time
Mix 1-2 Tbsp. essential oils into grains, vegetables, and meats daily	Essential oils help reduce inflammation and help maintain satiety
Good quality protein (meat, fish, fowl, eggs, dairy, and legumes)	Provides good protein and fats
Take digestive enzymes and HCL with meals	Helps to properly break down protein and high fiber foods in the stomach
Eat 6-8 servings of a wide variety of brightly colored vegetables	Vegetables are low in calories; you will not gain weight; provides vitamins, minerals, phytochemicals, antioxidants which are crucial for optimal health
Sprouts	High quality concentrated nutrients
Sea vegetables	Rich in trace minerals, good quality vegetable protein, easily digested

Monounsaturated fats	Used for low heat cooking; put a little water in the pan before the oil to keep the oil from getting too hot
Fresh and raw nuts and seeds (soaked in water) - store in freezer	Good source of essential fatty acids
Acceptable - Use in Moderation	
Whole unrefined grains (exclude wheat)	Provides sustained energy and nutrients. Caution: Take it easy as a breakfast food. Some people may need to avoid grains for breakfast.
Limited intake of fruits	Maintain blood sugar and insulin balance
Polyunsaturated fats (corn, safflower, sunflower, peanut oil)	Never cook with these oils, add after the food is cooked. Provides essential fatty acids

Plan Meals Using the Glycemic Index

The glycemic index (GI) provides a measure of the blood-sugar stress individual foods create. Controlling blood sugar is one key pillar in creating a successful diet for Adrenal Fatigue Syndrome, diabetes, hypoglycemia, and anti-aging. Elevated blood sugar is a direct reflection of high-sugar intake, so the ability of identifying low-sugar foods is important.

Eating low GI foods promotes an even flow of glucose into the blood. If you happen to eat a high GI food, such as puffed rice, we recommend adding a low glycemic index food such as nuts or whole milk yogurt. Doing so produces a balance between the high and low GI foods.

In Appendix B, you'll see a table of the glycemic index number for some common foods. These numbers use glucose as a baseline, using 100 as the value; all other values are relative to glucose.

To reduce blood sugar stress, focus on foods with *an index at or below 70.* Those with hypoglycemia type symptoms should focus on food with an index at or below 60. As indicated, always balance a higher GI food with a lower GI value food. You'll notice that meats, poultry, fish, eggs, seeds, and nuts are protein- and fat-containing foods and are automatically low GI foods.

Table Salt vs. Sea Salt

We recommend using sea salt because it contains additional trace minerals. Iodized table salt contains many additives that tax the body. Vegetable juice diluted with water and sprinkled with sea salt and kelp powder is a good fluid cocktail for AFS sufferers. Kelp contains about 90 mg of potassium and over 200 mg of sodium per serving and is easily absorbed.

Key Points to Remember

- A poor diet is a key leading cause of Adrenal Fatigue Syndrome and a trigger of adrenal crashes.
- Those in Stage 3 AFS must follow strict dietary guidelines; however,those with milder forms or those wishing to prevent Adrenal Fatigue Syndrome will do well by following the same dietary plan.
- All meals should be moderate in size and best planned using low-glycemic index foods.
- Frequent meals are needed for those prone to hypoglycemia.
- Simple sugar should be avoided, and moderate carbohydrates should be part of the meal plan that is balanced to offer quick energy.
- Avoid food high in caffeine and potassium.
- Soy should be consumed in moderation at best, due to its effect on the thyroid and ovaries.
- Adequate protein and good fats are necessary. Daily diet should include 30-40 percent above-the-ground vegetables, 10-20 percent whole grains, 10-15 percent whole fruits, 10-20 percent beans and legumes, 20-30 percent good fats, nuts, and seeds, and 20-30 percent animal foods.

Again, the minimum numbers add up to 100 percent, but the range represents varying diets day-to-day.

Chapter 2

Soups and Juicing for Health

Your mother is right. Soups are an excellent source of nutrients when you come down with flu or a cold. Chicken soup, for example, has been used for centuries to deliver nutrients during illnesses, and for good reasons. During flu and other illnesses, the body automatically slows down the digestion process in order to conserve energy to fight unwanted bacteria. Those with advanced Adrenal Fatigue Syndrome face similar problems—and worse. Instead of lasting a few days as a normal flu would, poor assimilation can go on for years and decades. This is compounded if you have food allergies and sensitivities. Soups offer a gentle and nurturing way to restore adrenal health, especially when other modes may not be well tolerated. Those with Stage 3C and beyond may find soups lifesaving, sparing the AFS sufferer an admission to the hospital for TPN (total parenteral nutrition).

We also offer guidelines for vegetable juicing, which is beneficial for many patients. However, the benefits of both the easy-to-make soups and juicing are not limited to those with AFS, but are part of any sound prevention program and anti-aging effort. In other words, these soups and juicing are good for the whole family.

Chicken Broth Recipes

Homemade chicken broth provides vital basic and foundational macronutrients sorely needed in advanced AFS recovery. We consider it an important part of our complete program that includes diet and lifestyle changes, along with carefully selected micronutrients, such as vitamins. Chicken bone and its marrow provide key nutrients, easily assimilated by the GI tract, and thus made bioavailable to the cells when delivered in a liquid form like broth. We recommend making the chicken broth fresh every morning so it's ready to be consumed from mid-day onwards for the rest of the day.

Below are three recipes that are easy to follow and produce excellent broth.

Note: Do not substitute these ingredients with commercial off-the-shelf products, because many contain MSG and are too diluted to have any significant clinical impact.

Each cup (8 fl oz) of our homemade chicken broth provides:

- **20 calories;**
- **1 gram carbohydrates;**
- **3 grams protein;**
- **0.5 grams of fat; 0 grams of saturated fat; 0 grams of cholesterol.**

The nutritional value goes far beyond what meets the eye; it rests with the bone marrow. Bone marrow is the essence of all mammals and contains all of the necessary nutrients for the human body, such as proteins, vitamins, B complex, and minerals (calcium, magnesium, zinc). Bone marrow also contains *lecithin* (a fatty substance occurring widely in animal and plant foods and a building block for other chemicals in the body) and *methionine* (an essential amino acid). It has been used as a whole food source since early civilization. Studies show it helps maintain healthy cholesterol levels, reduces inflammation, and promotes a strong immune system that is tied to the adrenal glands.

As we've said, most individuals suffering from Adrenal Fatigue Syndrome have salt cravings as well as fluid depletion. Drinking chicken broth helps restore fluid volume, and adding salt to chicken broth is an excellent way to replenish sodium in the body. We place no restriction on the amount of added salt, provided no signs of edema or high blood pressure are present and if your private physician approves.

Those who have a tendency to urinate in the middle of the night should restrict fluid intake in the evening to avoid excessive fluid buildup and urine retention in the bladder, which then leads to nighttime urination.

Our recommendation is to drink one cup (8 oz.) chicken broth twice a day, preferably midmorning and mid-afternoon, times that the body often runs out of steam. At these times, chicken broth can recharge the body. If you can only drink the broth once a day, then have it at the time of your worst low-point of energy. Three common lowest energy times are midmorning, mid afternoon, or immediately after work. You can also add a cup of chicken broth after exercising.

For those recovering from AFS, we recommend doing adrenal exercises (See Chapter 6, *Adrenal Fatigue Syndrome and Healing Exercise*) midmorning followed by a cup of chicken broth and a small healthy snack.

Some individuals with severe AFS need a more aggressive nourishment protocol. These individuals should have a cup of chicken broth five times a day, preferably:

- in the morning right after waking up (using the leftover broth from the previous day is acceptable as a matter of practicality)

- freshly prepared chicken broth at midmorning
- with lunch
- early afternoon (two hours after lunch)
- late afternoon (4-5 PM)

Again, for maximum effectiveness, before you drink the broth do short sessions of Adrenal Breathing Exercises (8-24 breaths lasting 1-3 minutes), designed to help stimulate the parasympathetic nervous system and thus prepare the GI track for optimum assimilation of nutrients into the bloodstream.

If desired, you can add some raw nuts along with the broth as a snack. The protein and fat from the nuts enhance sustained energy release; the salted broth will generate an immediate energy boost. In addition, you can take your adrenal supplements at the same time as the broth.

For maximum benefit, follow these guidelines:

- Make the broth fresh daily in the morning, rotating the three recipes, thus making a different recipe each day.

- Drink the broth warm to hot as tolerated, one cup each time.

- Reheat on your stove top, not in a microwave.

- Each recipe makes 3-5 cups, but the longer you boil it, the less liquid remains.

- You can have 2-6 ounces of the chicken meat before bedtime, along with some nuts, to combat sleep onset or sleep maintenance insomnia. (See Chapter 5, *Adrenal Fatigue Syndrome and Healing Sleep.*)

Remove the skin and fat from the chicken before making the broth; if some oil remains after boiling, skim it off with a spoon or a shredded paper towel.

Note: As you will see, the recipes and instructions are essentially identical except for the vegetable choices in each.

Chicken Broth Recipe 1

1/2 chicken, skin and fat removed. Use all the bone. The breast meat can be saved for other uses, but use the bones for the broth.

1 medium onion, chopped
2-3 stalks of celery cut in 3-inch segments
1 medium carrot chopped

Add enough water to cover the chicken and vegetables, plus three more inches.

Bring to a boil, and then decrease heat to medium and cook for 30 minutes. Then reduce heat to medium-low for another 90 minutes.

Carefully remove the chicken to remove the meat from the bones, and then drain the vegetables to make a broth.

Salt to taste before serving.

Chicken Broth Recipe 2

Instead of carrots, use:
1 medium beet root, peeled and chopped

Chicken Broth Recipe 3

Instead of carrots, use:
One 6-10 inch lotus root peeled and chopped

Juicing

Juicing tends to be one of those health recommendations that many people are attracted to, but it seems both expensive and a lot of work. However, we recommend reviving your interest in juicing because of the many benefits listed below.

Three general categories of juices exist: green juices, vegetable juices, and fruit juices. We emphasize green and vegetable juices for those in advanced AFS, and recommend limiting fruit juices to those who are in mild stages of AFS only.

Benefits of Vegetable Juicing

The benefits to vegetable juicing are many if the body can tolerate it. They include:

- Easy to digest and absorb.
- Enzymes, vitamins, minerals, and phytochemicals remain intact and active and in much larger quantities than if the piece of vegetable is eaten whole.
- Flushes out acid wastes and detoxifies the liver to improve clearance of byproducts.
- Improves the immune system.
- Rich in chlorophyll.
- Cleansing, rejuvenating, and energizing.

Note: Do not start juicing on your own without professional supervision if you have advanced AFS. Improper juicing can worsen AFS and trigger adrenal crashes.

Buying and Preparation Tips for Vegetable Juicing:

- Don't buy more than a week's worth of fresh fruits and vegetables, for they may spoil before you use them.
- Buy organic produce if possible.
- Thoroughly wash the produce before juicing. Use a vegetable brush to remove any residue and waxes. (You may also want to use vegetable washes that are found in health food stores.). Let the produce sit in a tub of clean water filled with activated charcoals for 20 minutes. Store the cleaned vegetables in containers to keep the freshness.
- When using potatoes for juicing, avoid those with a green tint. The green coloring is caused by a chemical called solanine. It can cause diarrhea, vomiting, and abdominal pain. Also, remove any sprouts or eyes on them.
- Stems and leaves of most vegetables can be left intact when juicing, except for carrot and rhubarb greens which must be removed.
- To make leafy green vegetable juices (spinach, lettuce, greens, etc.) more palatable, mix them with ½ carrot, 1 slice apple, or ¼ beet root.
- As a general rule, don't mix vegetables and fruits together when juicing.
- Strong tasting vegetables such as broccoli, onions, and rutabaga should be used sparingly.
- Garlic is a wonderful, immune building addition to your juices. Before juicing your garlic, it must be immersed

in vinegar for one minute to destroy any bacteria and mold on the surface. Those with a sensitive stomach may need to avoid this.

- Stop the vegetable juicing if you feel more wired or tired.

Juicing Machines

The best juicing machine is the cold press. Reputable brands include Green Machine, Omega, or Champion. But for the adrenal recovery process, if budget is a concern, a regular centrifuge type of juicer will serve the purpose.

Quantity

Not everyone can tolerate juicing. We recommend starting slow, with two ounces in the morning on an empty stomach every other day, or as directed. Increase the frequency to daily slowly as tolerated over a few weeks. Increase by one ounce per week until you reach 8 ounces daily. Excessive juicing is not recommended in advanced AFS because of the risk of developing re-toxification or die-off reaction as toxins tend to recirculate in the body.

Good Vegetables for Juicing

Base vegetables for juicing –1 celery stalk, ¼ carrot, 4 lettuce leaves

Add two of the following for variety:

- alfalfa sprouts
- cucumber
- beet greens
- dandelion greens
- parsley
- endive

- spinach
- lettuce (romaine, red leaf, green leaf, etc.)
- cilantro
- wheatgrass
- barley greens
- pumpkin
- sweet potato, potatoes
- bitter melon / bitter gourd
- summer squash

Cruciferous vegetables such as:

- bok choy
- mustard greens
- kale
- cabbage (red, green, napa, etc.)
- watercress
- collard greens
- turnip root and greens
- arugula
- radish, daikon
- broccoli, cauliflower
- kohlrabi
- Brussels sprouts

Note: Those who have estrogen dominance and thyroid issues should avoid cruciferous vegetables.

Preparation Tips for Fruit Juicing

While we generally do not recommend fruit juicing for those with advanced AFS, juicing can be part of a recovery program when AFS is mild or if there are no hypoglycemic issues. Proper preparation is the key to an effective juicing program. Here are some tips:

- Wash and prepare the fruits as you did the vegetables.
- Fruit juicing should be done in a blender so you also get the benefit of the fibers.
- Remove the skin before juicing apricots, grapefruits, kiwis, oranges, papaya, peaches, and pineapples.
- As a rule, leave small seeds in the fruits, except apple seeds, which contain cyanides. Therefore, remove all apple seeds before juicing.
- Always add a serving of whey protein and a few soaked raw nuts (you don't need to soak cashews or macadamia nuts) to fruit juice. This modulates the effect of the sugar content.
- Add 1-2 cups of water to dilute the thickness of the fruit juice so you can drink it.
- Rotate the fruits used daily—always have 1 berry, and 2 other fruits.
- The best time to have fruit juice is around 3-4 PM when your blood sugar is the lowest.

Whether they are from fruit or vegetables, fresh juices you make in your own kitchen are the best quality and are our first choice for juicing. However, we realize that juicing is time consuming and difficult for some. Fortunately, fresh organic juice blends are available in refrigerated cases in many supermarkets today. Those with AFS can fill in with these commercial blends if home juicing is not an option. Because nutrients are lost if they sit around too long, it's best to drink the juice immediately after making it.

Key Points to Remember

- Soups are an important way to deliver macronutrients to those with advanced AFS, as their gastric assimilation system is invariably compromised.
- Chicken broth is particularly nutritious and is easily absorbed, making it ideal for those in a weakened state.
- Juicing vegetables can be detoxifying, but aggressive use can lead to excessive re-toxification or die-off reactions. In those who are compromised, this can precipitate adrenal crashes.
- Fruit juices should be avoided except when AFS is mild.

Chapter 3

Food and Chemical Sensitivities

Sensitivities, sometimes loosely referred to as allergies, are a worldwide phenomenon. For example, allergies to peanuts, dairy, and wheat are very common and often show up in allergy testing. However, we can't rely on testing alone to establish such sensitivities. As in other situations discussed throughout this book, laboratory testing often shows a normal result, but the medical history and observations point to an abnormality or dysfunction. Sensitivity to wheat is often subtle—hidden—and a negative result on an allergy test isn't determinative. We discuss wheat sensitivity in detail because it's so widespread in Adrenal Fatigue Syndrome.

We also offer guidelines for vegetable juicing, which is beneficial for many patients. However, the benefits of both the easy-to-make soups and juicing are not limited to those with AFS, but are part of any sound prevention program and anti-aging effort. In other words, these soups and juicing are good for the whole family.

Wheat in the Modern Era

After maize and rice, wheat is the third most produced cereal. Wheat has been around a long time, too. Domestically cultivated since 9,000 B.C., the human civilization would look drastically different had it not been for wheat, an inexpensive staple food much of the world relies on for energy. Wheat products include flour used for many thousands of varieties of breads, breakfast cereals, pasta/noodles, plus many kinds of cookies and cakes. Fermented wheat is used to make beer and other alcoholic drinks, and it's the base of some biofuels. It's no exaggeration to say that in many parts of the world, wheat, in all its forms, is a sunrise to sundown food and more recently, a fuel.

Unfortunately, the wheat of today differs from wheat of ancient times. Over the past several decades, the drive to increase production has ushered in an era in which food scientists have developed technological advances designed to lower cost, extend shelf life, and increase variety, while also increasing production. Wheat producers and processors have achieved their goals through hybridization. Wheat has been selectively bred to produce larger quantities of lectin protein, a type of wheat germ agglutinin (WGA), and glycoprotein.

This manipulation of the wheat plant is not without negative consequences. For example, hybridization has greatly increased the amount of gluten protein now found in wheat. It is estimated that lectins are present in about 30 percent of the western diet. Today's pure wheat flour is processed into refined white flour. The principal parts of wheat and white flour are gluten and starch. The problem begins when lectins bind to the sugar in cells in the gut and blood, initiating a cascade of inflammatory responses. Scientific literature shows that dietary lectins can drastically reduce natural killer (NK) cell activity directly and through disruption of intestinal flora. Natural killer cells are one of the body's most vital defenses against unwelcomed bacteria and virus.

Lectins in the human body appear on the vascular endothelial lining in order for blood cells to escape into the tissue. (Lectins should not be confused with leptin, an endocrine hormone.) They are also present in the liver to help capture microorganisms. Finally, lectins act as a defense system by coating foreign antigens, making them more susceptible to destruction by the body's immune driven cells. Lectins, however, have a dark side. We now understand that lectin proteins found in wheat are often the primary cause of many of today's illnesses and allergies. WGA lectin has the potential to:

- damage major tissues of the body
- promote inflammation
- impede digestion and absorption
- disrupt bacteria balance
- disturb endocrine function

WGA lectin proteins are also capable of circulating in the blood and crossing the blood-brain barrier. Lectin itself also acts to defend the wheat plant from its natural enemies, such as fungi and insects, which is why lectin has been bred into the plant in modern times. Ever increasing production is the goal, and the hardier the plant, the greater the production.

Lectins are also called agglutinins because of their ability to bind to many cell surfaces, causing agglutination (cell clumping) reactions. Lectins bind to sugar on the cell membrane, proteins, and fat.

Because this protein lectin is very small and difficult to break down and is virtually resistant to digestion, it hampers normal biological processes and is stored in important tissues, thereby acting as an *anti-nutrient.*

Usually, sprouting and fermenting, or the process of digesting grains, can work against some anti-nutrient effects. However, lectins are resilient proteins and resist these processes; lectins may even subsist in sprouted breads, which are purported to be a healthier form of wheat.

WGA lectin is very hard to break down because it is formed by the same chemical bonds that produce vulcanized rubber and human hair, both of which are tough, flexible, and durable. WGA lectin has unique properties in that it has the potential to directly harm most of the body's tissues even in a body that has no evidence of genetic or immune system susceptibilities. This might be one reason why chronic inflammatory and degenerative conditions are endemic to wheat consuming populations. What is surprising is that WGA is found in its highest concentration in "whole wheat." The push toward more whole grain bread may actually promote the onslaught of lectin-driven illnesses. While most healthy people are not affected, those with AFS are particularly vulnerable.

Foods with the highest concentrations of lectin include all dried beans (especially soy), grains of all kinds (especially wheat), seeds and nuts, dairy, and plants in the nightshade family (i.e., white potatoes and tomatoes). The large concentrations of lectin in plant seeds decreases with growth, so sprouting the grains and seeds before eating reduces the lectin concentration. However, avoiding soy, wheat, and dairy is the best action. Soaking nuts for at least twenty-four hours improves their digestibility.

Threats of Wheat Lectin

Exactly how does lectin harm your health? Lectin:

- **Promotes inflammation:** Even at minor concentrations, WGA lectins stimulate the production of pro-inflammatory chemical messengers.
- **Is toxic to the immune system:** WGA lectin may fasten to and stimulate white blood cells.

- **Is toxic to the nervous system:** WGA lectin easily passes through the blood-brain barrier and binds to the myelin sheath that protects the nerve. It can also inhibit the nerve growth factor, which is important for growth, maintenance, and survival of certain target neurons.
- **Is toxic to the cells:** WGA lectin has the capacity to induce programmed cell death.

WGA lectin enters the body through the intestinal membranes, which then allows it to circulate in your body.

Almost everyone has antibodies to some dietary lectins in the body. Many food allergies and delayed food sensitivities are actually immune system reactions to lectin. Ultimately, our intrinsic constitution will determine to a large degree how we respond. The weaker the body, the more problematic this becomes. It should come as no surprise that those with advanced AFS are particularly vulnerable to lectin sensitivity due to their low gastric assimilation and clearance capability.

Looking at Wheat Gluten

Gluten originates from the Latin word for glue, implying the bonding properties that bind or hold together wheat products, such as cake and bread. These qualities might be advantageous to cooks and bakers, but they are also responsible for standing in the way of effective breakdown and absorption of nutrients. Eating gluten results in a constipated lump in the gut rather than a nutritious, easily digested meal. This lump of undigested gluten then provokes the immune system to launch an attack on the lining of the small intestine, leading to symptoms such as diarrhea or constipation, nausea, and stomach aches. As time passes, the small intestine becomes more injured, making it harder to absorb certain nutrients such as calcium and iron. This in turn leads to osteoporosis, anemia, and other problems.

Two Types of Allergies

You might be aware that two kinds of food allergies exist. At times, individuals are severely allergic and have serious immediate anaphylactic reactions (a reaction commonly associated with peanuts and shellfish, for example) characterized by respiratory symptoms. This is a "true allergy." When most people hear the words "food allergy," they associate them with the severe and sudden anaphylactic response.

The second type of food allergy is much more common and far less understood by the general public. It is referred to as an IgG food intolerance, food sensitivity, or delayed food allergy, better known as delayed food sensitivity. IgG is the type of allergy to wheat, dairy, and soy we see at work in AFS. Delayed food sensitivity brings many different types of reactions, which may take place hours or even days after you've eaten the offending foods.

You may be unaware that some of our physical problems are related to foods you consume, much less foods you ate three days ago. If you do associate a physical response with something you ate, you usually try to think of an unusual food. But you're most likely reacting to a food (or foods) you eat regularly. Allergies to wheat, dairy, and soy are among the most common culprits within the universe of delayed food allergy, largely because they comprise so much of the average diet. At times, you can be sensitive to a specific combination of foods that you don't react to individually, or a certain food was okay, but overnight you become sensitive to the same food.

Conditions and Symptoms Associated with Delayed Food Sensitivity

Aside from the obvious gastric symptoms (indigestion, diarrhea, constipation, and so forth), delayed food allergies can also manifest themselves in ways most people would never think to connect. Examples include: rheumatoid arthritis, migraine headaches, asthma, attention deficit disorder (ADD), autism, fibromyalgia, and other autoimmune syndromes. All these and many other conditions have food sensitivity triggers, and those who have identified their food sensitivities and eliminated them from their diets see dramatic improvements in their health.

Day to day complaints can also be caused by delayed food allergies. Consider this list of seemingly ordinary symptoms:

- cloudy thinking/inability to concentrate
- lethargy/fatigue
- headaches, including migraines
- joint pain
- muscle weakness
- depression
- chronic sinus issues/plugged ears or chronic ear infections
- weight gain
- dark circles under the eyes, red/ruddy cheeks/acne
- cravings for the allergenic foods
- itchy mouth and ears, or feeling itchy all over the body

Wheat and Adrenal Fatigue Syndrome

Because of the high frequency of wheat allergy or intolerance, it plays an especially important role in Adrenal Fatigue

Syndrome. Among those with AFS, the slow onset food intolerance is the most common type of allergy. It is characterized by delayed subclinical allergic reactions that can take hours or days to manifest symptoms. However, at times we might not even recognize a reaction, or we attribute it to another cause.

Such delayed reactions include:

- low energy
- dry skin, itchiness
- heart palpitations
- blurry vision
- irritability/anxiety
- irritable bowel syndrome (IBS)

Normally, we don't see hives and respiratory difficulties typical of *acute* allergic responses.

As you can see, these delayed symptoms are rather general, which is why their potential link to wheat is overlooked, even though wheat is omnipresent in everyday diets of many millions of individuals. Unlike acute responses, these general symptoms typically develop in a stealth manner and gradually worsen over years. This is one reason conventional doctors fail to connect these symptoms to wheat. Unfortunately, this kind of allergy does not show up during allergy testing and remains subclinical. In other words, as an allergy, wheat can elude detection while it causes havoc in an already weak adrenal system.

As with other allergic responses, cortisol is the key hormone regulating the response. In Adrenal Fatigue Syndrome, cortisol output first rises in the early stages, but eventually falls, a progression that usually takes place over years of chronic stress. As Adrenal Fatigue Syndrome progresses, cortisol output reduces and allergic responses become more symptomatic.

As discussed earlier, lectin sensitivity is a major contributor to this problem. It is often accompanied by sensitivity to other foods, such as soy and dairy. As the adrenals weaken, multiple food sensitivities become prevalent. In addition to food allergies, we also see multiple chemical sensitivities.

Food intolerance weakens the body, especially the lining of the stomach and intestines, which means that the body expends more energy than normal to assimilate and metabolize foods. Then, the already stressed adrenals are unable to maintain the energy supply to the body. As this downhill process continues, the GI tract typically becomes irritated and inflamed, and over time, the continuous irritation leads to stomach pain, heartburn, gas, and/or other uncomfortable digestive symptoms. In addition, it's possible to develop leaky gut syndrome, which occurs with increased permeability of the intestinal walls. This means that undigested proteins and fats leak out of the intestine and into the bloodstream, where they set off an autoimmune reaction. This irritation triggers a further increase in demand for the adrenals to produce more cortisol to calm the inflammation. However, this occurs at a time when the adrenals are already stressed.

What You Can Do

Fortunately, you can prevent or reverse delayed food allergy or intolerance. The best way is to eliminate the offending food from your diet while you also normalize adrenal function. Then, as adrenal function improves, the body's ability to combat food intolerance also improves, and these allergens cause fewer symptoms. As time passes, many people are able to tolerate the allergenic foods, and provided the adrenal functions are normalized, these individuals no longer have problems with the foods that once caused so much trouble.

Gluten Free or Wheat Free

As a larger issue, however, most people would live healthier lives if they stopped eating wheat, and perhaps other refined grains. Even those without gluten intolerance tend to feel better when they eliminate wheat and other grains. The reason is that grains break down into sugar in the body and elevate insulin levels, which are linked to many other health problems, including obesity, high cholesterol, high blood pressure, type 2 diabetes and cancer. In other words, with or without obvious reasons and consequences, wheat-free diets have health benefits.

AFS and Gluten

As a preventive measure, everyone with Adrenal Fatigue Syndrome should eliminate wheat from their diet (along with dairy). This sounds easy enough, but wheat now hides in many foods including soy sauce, soups, cold cuts (processed deli meats), candies, and certain low-fat or nonfat products. Read labels carefully and avoid other starches and additives, some of which may be derived from wheat. These include:

- malt
- hydrolyzed vegetable protein (HVP)
- texturized vegetable protein (TVP)
- natural flavorings
- some pharmaceuticals
- alcohol

The following is a (long!) list of common products that may contain wheat, essentially any products that contain flour, bran, wheat germ, wheat starch, or gluten, including:

- baked goods, including bagels, biscuits and rolls, doughnuts, cakes and pies of all types, cookies, and muffins
- bread and bread crumbs, crackers and cracker meal, packaged stuffing
- pancakes and waffles (homemade or packaged mixes), breakfast cereals
- pasta (macaroni, spaghetti, lasagna, and egg noodles)
- breaded meat, fish, and poultry, plus deep fried foods (chicken, fish, vegetables, cheese sticks, and so forth)
- ice cream cones and ice cream sandwiches
- hot dogs, luncheon meats, and pizza
- products containing malt
- coffee substitutes
- bottled salad dressing (unless labeled gluten free)
- gravy, sauces that have been thickened but are opaque (e.g. cream sauces)
- most prepared cream soups
- soy sauce

The Practical Approach

At least at first, it can be difficult to cut out all wheat products in your diet, although today, many alternatives and substitutes exist. First, avoid the most obvious foods, such as bread and pasta, for a couple of weeks. Then eliminate crackers, cakes, cookies, pies, and other desserts. It may take you up to six months to get over your cravings for wheat products. That is normal. However, as your body detoxifies and gains strength because you have avoided wheat, you will notice ill effects if you reintroduce wheat into your diet.

Good alternatives: Today, an increasing number of wheat-free/gluten-free foods, from bread to salad dressing, are available in health food stores and regular supermarkets. In addition, brown rice products, such as rice flour bread and other products are appropriate for both vegetarians and non-vegetarians. You also can use sprouted breads (Ezekiel bread) or gluten-free bread for toast or sandwiches. Rice flour wraps are also good substitutes for bread. You can also use other rice and rice flour products, oat flour, kamut, and quinoa. Those who have cravings for carbohydrates will not necessarily see any difference by using gluten-free products.

If you begin eating some of these wheat containing foods again, you may note that your body isn't reacting well to them, which provides additional incentive to stay away from wheat.

Multiple Chemical Sensitivities

Many individuals develop sensitivities to substances other than food. We see this developing frequently among those with Adrenal Fatigue Syndrome. For example, along with being environmentally unfriendly, commercial household cleaning products are also highly toxic to many people. In order to avoid these products, we've listed some common, safe, and environmentally friendly cleaners to use around the house.

- Baking soda—can clean, scour, and deodorize, and it can even soften water.
- Borax—also known as sodium borate, works like baking soda and can even clean wallpaper and painted walls.

- White vinegar—especially good for removing grease, mildew, odors, stains, and wax build up.
- Citrus solvent—good for removing oil and grease, and can clean paint brushes as well.
- Lemon oil—effective against many bacteria found in homes.
- Isopropyl alcohol—an excellent disinfectant.
- Cornstarch—use to shampoo carpets and rugs, and also to polish furniture.

Your home floors are often in direct contact with the soles of your feet; use these floor cleaners and polishes to keep your body safe:

- **Wood**: Use a one-to-one ratio of vinegar and vegetable oil. Apply a thin coat on the floor and rub in well.
- **Painted wood:** Mix 1 teaspoon of washing soda with 1 gallon of hot water and clean.
- **Brick and stone tiles:** Mix 1 cup of white vinegar with 1 gallon water and clean, then rinse with clear water.
- **Varnished wood:** Add a couple drops of lemon oil into a half cup of warm water. Pour into a spray bottle and shake well. Spray onto cloth and wipe. Finish by wiping furniture again with a dry soft cotton cloth.
- **Unvarnished wood:** Mix 2 teaspoons of olive oil and 2 teaspoons of lemon juice and apply using wide strokes.

Keeping so many products can be a handful, so try out these all-purpose cleaner formulas you can make yourself:

- **For all purpose general cleaning:** Mix a quarter cup of baking soda with a half cup of vinegar into a half gallon of water. This mixture can be stored for a while. It is useful for bathroom cleaning such as the removal of water deposit stains on and around shower stalls, windows, mirrors, and chrome fixtures.
- **For laundry:** Mix 1 cup of Ivory® soap or Fels Naptha® soap with ½ cup of washing soda and ½ cup of borax. Use 1 tablespoon for lighter loads and 2 tablespoons for heavier loads.
- **For bathroom mold:** 1 part 3 percent hydrogen peroxide with 2 parts water in a spray bottle. Spray on affected areas and wait for 1 hour before rinsing.
- **For carpet stains:** Use equal parts white vinegar and water and mix in a spray bottle. Apply directly on the stain and let sit for several minutes before cleaning with a brush and warm soapy water.
- **For really tough carpet stains:** Mix a quarter cup each of salt, borax, and vinegar to form a paste. Rub the paste into the carpet and leave for a couple of hours before vacuuming.

These household remedies have the advantage of being simple and eco-friendly. Most people find that once they begin using these safe products, they have no desire to return to the harsh cleaning products that will one day fade into the past.

In the next chapter, we address another key component of recovery, which is how to get a good night's sleep. Sleep disturbances plague so many with AFS.

Key Points to Remember

- Food and chemical sensitivity is very common in those with AFS, especially those in advanced stages.
- Wheat and dairy products are the main culprits of delayed food sensitivity. Everyone with AFS should try to reduce or eliminate wheat from their diet.
- WGA lectin found within wheat is linked to a variety of inflammatory reactions within the body.
- Gluten, found in most grains, triggers sensitivities to the digestive system.
- We are exposed to many chemicals that are toxic to the adrenal glands. Commercial cleaning products are especially common. Fortunately, there are many natural alternatives to these chemicals, including the use of vinegar and baking soda.

Chapter 4

Adrenal Fatigue Syndrome, Insomnia and Healing Sleep

Insomnia is a classic sign of Adrenal Fatigue Syndrome, and is usually a result of the malfunction of the hypothalamic-pituitary-adrenal (HPA) hormonal axis, over-activation of central nervous system neurotransmitters such as norepinephrine, and imbalances with the sympathetic nervous system and adrenal medullary hormonal system (AHS) discussed in Chapter 2, *Stress, Hormone Basics and the "Forgotten" Adrenals.* Rather than being a single, discrete condition, insomnia in AFS more closely resembles a complex condition, because it is quite different from regular insomnia experienced by healthy individuals. The main complaints include part or, frequently, all of the following:

- difficulty falling asleep (sleep onset insomnia, or SOI)
- disturbed sleep and being easily awakened at night
- difficulty falling back to sleep (sleep maintenance insomnia, or SMI)
- seldom or never feeling rested, leading to morning fatigue, a slower morning start, and feeling fatigued during the day

Sleep Onset Insomnia (SOI)

Most people think of SOI, a situation in which it's difficult to fall asleep, as what insomnia is all about. In fact, it is only one manifestation of insomnia. For normal sleep to occur, and to awaken refreshed and energized, it's important that cortisol be at its highest level in the morning and at its lowest level at night. When the cortisol balance is off, sleep patterns can be affected. High cortisol levels are typical of people suffering from mild Adrenal Fatigue Syndrome. This happens when the adrenals are on overdrive, putting out excessive cortisol throughout the day in order to deal with constant stress. Some of the excess cortisol carries into the night and affects the ability to fall asleep, thus contributing to SOI. Lack of sleep is also a trigger that further increases cortisol output, which in turn worsens insomnia. This forms a vicious cycle.

At the same time, stress and insomnia trigger the AHS. The adrenal medulla is activated to produce adrenaline, which is, as you recall, a hormone responsible for the fight-or-flight response. A high adrenaline level can independently disturb sleep patterns by putting the body on full alert, commonly referred to as being wired. Besides, when the body is on full alert, as is expected and advantageous during threats of danger and other emergencies, sleep is the last thing the body needs. The problem arises when adrenaline is high when no immediate danger is at hand. High cortisol and high adrenaline can occur simultaneously, a common situation among those who suffer from Adrenal Fatigue Syndrome. On top of this, the brain usually is already on overdrive with norepinephrine overload, leading to a concurrent state of constant arousal. This situation is made worse if stimulatory natural compounds are used such as certain vitamins, herbs, and glandulars. It comes as no surprise that advancing AFS often equates to worsening insomnia.

Below are some general tips to help you fall asleep more easily:

- ***Sleep in a cool and completely quiet and dark room.*** A dark room enhances the production of *melatonin*, an important sleep regulating hormone. Draw and close all the window coverings; even a small amount of light in the environment can reduce melatonin output from the brain.
- ***Go to bed and get up at about the same time every day, even on weekends.*** Sticking to a schedule helps reinforce your body's sleep-wake cycle, and doing the same things each night tells your body that its time to wind down. This may include taking a warm bath or shower, reading a book, or listening to soothing music. Relaxing activities done with lowered lights can help ease the transition between wakefulness and sleepiness.
- ***Remove all electrical appliances, such as nightlights and alarm clocks.*** Put them at least ten feet away from the bed to reduce EMF (electromagnetic field) emission, which can alter sleep patterns.
- ***Do not do strenuous aerobic exercise or power yoga after dinner.*** You want to avoid over stimulating the SNS (sympathetic nervous system), which is frequently on overdrive in people who already suffer from Adrenal Fatigue Syndrome.
- ***Turn off your computer, TV, loud music, and hyper-stimulating video games.*** After 6:00 PM, these and similar devices can trigger an adrenaline rush. Try reading books in a quiet environment during the evening; if you do watch TV, then avoid channel surfing and don't watch violent action shows.

- ***Avoid adrenal stimulators.*** It's important to avoid certain foods and chemicals in order to avoid excessive stress on the adrenal glands. Stay away from sugary foods and both caffeinated and decaffeinated drinks of all kinds, along with other common offenders including nicotine, alcohol, allergic foods (histamine is an adrenal stimulant), green tea, and chocolate. In addition, you should avoid herbs and glandular products, unless approved by your healthcare professional. We also recommend avoiding partially hydrogenated fats, such as those used in deep fried foods and shortenings, which inhibit steroid hormone synthesis. Artificial sweeteners should be eliminated as well—they block the conversion of phenylalanine to tyrosine, which is needed to synthesize catecholamines (particular types of substances that function like hormones or neuro-transmitters) in the adrenal medulla. Non-stimulating herbal teas, such as chamomile, are permitted.

- ***Perform gentle Adrenal Restorative Exercises in the late afternoon*** (*discussed in the next chapter*). This helps the body transition from (presumably) the end of a work day to the evening. However, do not perform them in the evening. Low intensity aerobics, such as long, slow walks should be done in the morning or late in the afternoon. Taking a short walk after dinner is an exception, provided that the body does not feel drained immediately afterwards.

- ***Always go to sleep before 10 PM at the latest.*** If you are tired, go to sleep earlier. Do the Adrenal Breathing Exercises (addressed in the next chapter) just before bedtime and not at any other time in the evening.

This will help with the transition to sleep. Adrenal Breathing should always be part of your relaxing bedtime routine.

- ***A small snack of protein and fat (a handful of nuts or cottage cheese) before sleep is beneficial.*** A light snack before bed can help promote sleep, and pairing tryptophan-containing foods (such as turkey and certain dairy products) with carbohydrates, helps to calm the brain, which allows the body to sleep better.
- ***If you don't fall asleep, get up and do something like Adrenal Restorative Exercises or Adrenal Breathing Exercises.*** Go back to bed when you're tired, but don't agonize about falling asleep. The stress will only prevent sleep. It is common for many people with advanced AFS to feel wired and tired at the same time, so if your mind is racing and can't stop, use the energy to think positive thoughts. Try to set aside worries and negative thoughts and form the habit of engaging in positive thinking at bedtime. To the extent you can, occupy your mind with images of relaxing places or happy events.
- ***A good bed is subjective and different for each person.*** Make sure you have a comfortable bed that offers orthopedic comfort. If you share your bed, make sure there's enough room for two. Children and pets often disrupt sleep, so you may need to set limits on how often they can sleep in your bed with you.
- ***Take a natural sleep aid as directed by your healthcare professional.*** Many are available, and each has individual characteristics. Finding the right one or combination might require trial and error. We discuss this later on in this chapter.

Sleep Maintenance Insomnia (SMI)

Sleep maintenance insomnia involves the tendency to wake up in the middle of the night but be unable to go back to sleep. Usually, a number of factors trigger SMI. Metabolic imbalances, such as problems with blood sugar and insulin regulation, may occur during sleep and cause wakefulness. When the body must deal with excessive daytime stress, the body can sometimes fall asleep simply because the magnitude of the physical fatigue overwhelms high adrenaline and cortisol levels. The wired and tired body needs a break, so it crashes, allowing for a few hours of sleep. However, cortisol and adrenaline levels remain high during this time, and these sustained high levels in the middle of the night eventually awaken the body. The physical tiredness is reduced by a few hours of rest, leading to sleep maintenance insomnia. Once awakened, it is hard to fall back to sleep.

Those who suffer from advanced AFS often have concurrent metabolic imbalances, such as insulin dysregulation and subclinical hypoglycemia. When the body's glucose supplies (from food) are inadequate, the blood sugar level drops below a certain threshold level during sleep; this can activate the SNS and AHS, which leads to norepinephrine and adrenaline release, both of which can contribute to wakefulness.

By conventional laboratory standards the blood sugar level may be normal, but individuals may be extremely sensitive to the rollercoaster ride of the blood sugar level; even a small drop within normal ranges during the night can trigger awakening. These wakeful periods are often accompanied by symptoms such as heart palpitations and cold sweats. So, to avoid SMI we need to practice the aforementioned good sleep habits and follow the protocol for *SOI*, along with ensuring the stability of the blood glucose level throughout the evening. When your blood sugar level falls, healthy adrenals restore it back to normal. If the blood sugar levels are not stabilized, then we don't see optimal results when attempting to correct the adrenal status.

Below are dietary guidelines which are beneficial to both prevent and treat AFS, but also help stabilize both daytime and nighttime blood glucose levels. As you can see, they are much like the dietary guidelines listed in the previous chapter:

- ***Do not skip breakfast.*** In fact, it should be the biggest meal.
- ***Follow the mealtime guidelines for AFS***, being sure to eat every 2-3 hours during the day.
- ***Snack only on low glycemic foods***, such as nuts, seeds, hard-boiled eggs, and so forth. For sustained energy release, add a small amount of carbohydrate, such as a few raw carrot sticks to supply instant energy to the body.
- ***Avoid all fruit and vegetable juices.*** Whole fruit, such as apples, are acceptable.
- ***Never consume high glycemic fruits (or other foods) without a source of protein and fat to balance them.*** For example, a whole fruit along with some almond butter balances the carbohydrate of the fruit with protein and fat supplied by the almond butter spread.
- ***Take the prescribed natural compounds designed to stabilize blood sugar and calm the autonomic nervous system.*** Your healthcare professional will guide you on this.

- ***A bedtime snack is especially important.*** This snack may be a small portion of protein, carbohydrate, and fat, but for some, it may be nearly a full meal.
- ***If you wake up in the middle of the night, have another light snack to normalize blood sugar, thereby allowing you to go back to sleep.***

Sleep issues may take time to resolve, so begin by being patient. Stick with your routine and slowly but surely you will begin to experience the benefits of a good night's sleep.

Natural Sleep Aids

A great variety of sleep aids are available, but we know which work or don't work only through trial and error. Each sleep aid nutrient has specific pathways and affects individuals in different ways. For example:

- GABA (gamma-amino butyric acid, an amino acid that helps to regulate sleep and anxiety) works best for those with Adrenal Fatigue Syndrome and who are adrenal dominant.
- 5-HTP is usually more effective for the thyroid dominant type.

Because of individual reactions to different types of sleep aid nutrients and the predominance of paradoxical reactions in Adrenal Fatigue Syndrome, experienced clinicians use different combinations of natural compounds.

Considering Melatonin

Melatonin is a hormone produced by the pineal gland, located deep in the brain. Many older individuals use melatonin as a supplement and sleep aid because this hormone declines with age, thereby causing sleep disturbances in many people.

Although sleep patterns are often disrupted as we age, this reduction of the nightly release of melatonin by the pineal gland also occurs among those with AFS. Many individuals have discovered that bedtime doses of melatonin will restore their ability to have a sound and peaceful night's sleep. Taking oral melatonin helps with both SOI and SMI.

Low doses of melatonin (0.5 to 3 mg) act as a natural sleeping pill, but the dosages are individualized, especially with Adrenal Fatigue Syndrome. Trial and error is almost inevitable. We recommend starting with 0.5 to 1 mg, gradually increasing if there are no adverse side effects. The upper limits of dosage vary from person to person, and some need as much as 30 mg. A higher dose isn't necessarily better, however, and some people feel better on smaller doses.

When you first begin taking melatonin, you may feel slightly disoriented or dizzy during your first few waking hours. This hangover sensation should subside after a few nights of use. If it persists, then reduce the dose.

Note: High doses of melatonin are contraindicated in children, pregnant or nursing women, women trying to conceive, people taking prescription steroids, or who have mental illness, severe allergies, or immune system cancers such as lymphoma.

To effectively use melatonin, always take the hormone supplement just before bedtime. If you take it earlier in the daylight hours, it may disrupt sleeping and waking cycles. If you have a hangover sensation, then try taking melatonin earlier in the evening instead of at bedtime (but not during daytime hours).

Other Sleep Aids

If sleep continues to be a problem, other supplements and compounds might be helpful. For example, consider: phosphaditylserine, glutamine, magnesium, calcium, fish oil, progesterone, glutamine, theanine, flower remedies, herbs such as valerian, GABA, inosital, and 5-HTP (hydroxytryptophan). Interestingly, the herb, ashawandgha, may enhance sleep in some people for reasons not well understood.

It is not unusual for natural sleep aids to be grouped into a cocktail to work best. Those who are sensitive may need to be on a special schedule to avoid toxic metabolite buildup. Sometimes sleep improves but is short-lived. Other times, things can actually get worse, and then all of a sudden get better. Even in the best of hands, some trial and error is required.

Prescription Sleep Medication

Those who have unrelenting insomnia may need prescription sleep medication for a short time. However, proceed with extreme care and consider this only under close medical supervision because of potential addiction problems and the liver clearance complications frequently seen in those with advanced AFS. Nevertheless,

these prescription drugs are sometimes clinically necessary to help the body get much needed rest in order to reset itself during the recovery process. As much as we advise caution with these substances, their proper use can be of tremendous benefit.

Here, too, because each person reacts differently to prescription medications, expect a period of trial and error. Those with a weak constitution and high sensitivity must be on extra alert for paradoxical reactions, meaning that the action of the sleep medications leads to a state of hyperarousal.

We recommend starting at a very low dose. Those who are already on prescription sleep medication should not stop abruptly as sudden withdrawal can trigger adrenal crashes. The best time to reduce dependence on sleep medications is after adrenal reserves have been re-established. Many have reported a spontaneous reduction in insomnia as adrenal health returns. This is normal, and often reflects a reduction of the sympathetic overtone so common in adrenal exhaustion.

Sleep is so important for general health and for preventing and recovering from Adrenal Fatigue Syndrome that we recommend doing whatever you can to get a good night's sleep, both in duration and quality.

Key Points to Remember

- Most people with AFS complain of insomnia to some degree. The more advanced the AFS, the more serious this is.
- Sleep onset insomnia (SOI) is often due to an overflow of adrenaline or a cortisol imbalance in the body. A person usually feels wired-and-tired.
- Sleep maintenance insomnia (SMI) refers to the inability to fall back to sleep after waking up in the middle of the night. This can be due to a variety of metabolic and hormonal imbalances and this situation can be quite challenging.
- Most insomnia improves as Adrenal Fatigue Syndrome improves.
- Many sleep aids are available. Trial and error is required, and often a cocktail of natural sleep aids works the best.
- Melatonin is an excellent sleep aid. The dosage requirement varies greatly. Other important sleep aids include GABA, 5-HTP, magnesium, progesterone, and so forth.
- It is important to have good sleeping habits to facilitate restful sleep. The most important is to sleep in a completely quiet and dark room.

Chapter 5

Adrenal Fatigue Syndrome and Healing Exercise

Most people think of exercise in terms of *aerobic* activities, such as brisk walking, jogging, cycling, rowing, and other activities that elevate the heart rate and condition the cardiovascular system, or as *anaerobic*, such as strength training that builds and maintains muscles. These are beneficial to general good health, but fo r advanced Adrenal Fatigue Syndrome, they are not the best types of exercise. In fact, the wrong exercise program may make Adrenal Fatigue Syndrome worse and can easily trigger adrenal crashes. Let's look at the reasons for this dilemma.

One common misconception is that Adrenal Fatigue Syndrome equates to low energy only, which can be linked to the body's inability to overcome stress, whether it is physical, mental, or emotional. In addition, because all body functions require energy, low energy is the most prominent outcome in those with Adrenal Fatigue Syndrome. This sounds logical, but at the root level, however, AFS is much more complicated.

Think of a car running low on gas, plus it has a steering wheel problem, a gas pedal that continues to accelerate at will, and a brake pedal that malfunctions intermittently. In other words, many of the systems that ensure a smoothly running vehicle are broken. No longer under your control, the car is an accident waiting to happen—and it can't get you where you want to go. Translate these circumstances to your body and you are not far away from advanced Adrenal Fatigue Syndrome.

Like a car, the body needs to run smoothly for us to feel and perform well, which means we need perfect synchronization of numerous organs and systems. In AFS, the body is drained and low on energy, like a car running low on gas, and we see numerous concurrent imbalances. Since many hormones are dysregulated, low energy may exist with:

- hypoglycemia, low blood sugar, which we can liken to not enough gasoline in the gas tank
- feelings of being wired, like a sticky gas pedal that's stuck in acceleration
- foggy thinking, like a driver who texts while driving
- depression, which tells us the brake pedal has burned out

With the internal equilibrium of the body dysregulated, it is no wonder that the adrenals crash with each little stressor.

An Exercise Strategy

A successful Adrenal Recovery Exercise Program requires a strategy that helps you regain control of the core functions of the body. Returning to the analogy of the car, controlling the body involves more than adding gasoline to the tank. If the steering system is not functioning, you are still unable to get where you want to go, even with a full tank of gas. The goal is a complete rebalancing of the internal systems, so they can operate together smoothly and get you where you want to go. This involves a total mind-body approach incorporating lifestyle, exercise, diet, and nutrition, plus both mental and physical components. If done properly, exercise helps the adrenals boost their function, and thus, energy.

Energy and Exercise

Individuals in early AFS (Stages 1 and 2) may feel tired only intermittently and tend to quickly recover from any low energy state. As you recall from our discussion of the stages of AFS, those in advanced AFS (Stages 3 and 4) experience a constant low energy state and fatigue, which worsens over time. For those with advanced adrenal weakness, it is important to custom tailor an exercise program for the best use of limited energy.

Over-use of energy for exercise may trigger adrenal crashes. Therefore, it's of paramount importance to reach the right balance of intensity, length of exercise sessions, and frequency. Exercise makes many individuals in more advanced stages of AFS feel drained of energy, so they tend to avoid it. However, except during an adrenal crash, it's not beneficial to avoid exercise altogether. Other individuals treat their energy drain and fatigue by forcing themselves to do more and more. Both approaches can be wrong. This is why we recommend a personalized exercise program designed specifically for the level of adrenal function.

For vital organs to overcome a low energy state, we need to maintain a consistent energy stream, and any excess energy can be channeled into exercise. However, the amount of exercise must be adjusted to avoid over-stimulation of the fight-or-flight response mediated by epinephrine. The right exercise performed at the right time is tremendously beneficial, but the opposite is true as well. (See exercise graph in the next section.)

During the initial stages of healing advanced AFS, experienced clinicians want to conserve energy as much as possible, so the goal is *not to choose* exercises that are overly focused on increasing energy. A more gentle, nurturing approach starting from the core is more appropriate to increase internal reserves. After a comfortable level of reserve is accomplished and built up in the body, then over time, the body can go from a catabolic state into an anabolic state, in which muscles start to rebuild and strengthen. This level of healing must be accomplished gradually, step-by-step, which goes a long way in avoiding the common mistake in AFS recovery, over exercising.

A well designed Adrenal Recovery Exercise Program includes breathing, muscle toning, stretching, strength training, motion fluidity, control, and overall circulation. It considers the stage of AFS, the body's remaining reserve, the biological constitution, age, metabolic issues, past medical history, and injuries. (As with any exercise program, always consult and seek approval of your personal physician before beginning.)

The AFS Exercise Toolbox

Each tool has its place and must be deployed at the right time for maximum benefit. The proper program allows the body a total healing experience, starting at the cellular level in the core of the body. Remember, too, that the body has an internal repair system in place, and fortunately, the body is forgiving.

The tools are:

- Adrenal Breathing™ Exercises for basic harmony and ANS balance.
- Twelve Adrenal Restorative Exercises to enhance blood flow/oxygen delivery.
- Twenty-one Adrenal Yoga™ Exercise sessions, with three major components: the beginner phase, with a focus on breathing and stretching; the intermediate phase, with a focus on toning and strengthening; and the advanced phase, with a focus on fluidity and control.

In addition, we briefly describe *regular yoga, power yoga,* and *aerobics.* In this book, we're limiting our detailed discussion to the first two tools, but the graph below illustrates the way a comprehensive exercise program in stages can help restore the adrenal function and energy:

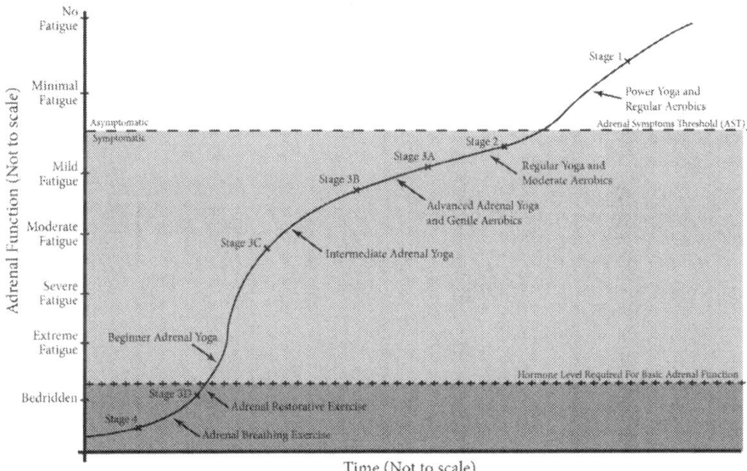

Figure 19. Adrenal Fatigue Syndrome Exercise Progression

Breathing as Therapy

Because breathing is an automatic function, the western medical world has not taken the time to understand its therapeutic significance. Only when breathing is compromised or obstructed is it considered and evaluated. Therefore, most people in the west are not taught the significance of proper breathing, let alone its healing power. As a result, the vast majority of people do not breathe properly, either while in a normal healthy state or when the body is weakened, as occurs with AFS.

Three main sets of muscles are active when you breathe normally: the intercostal muscles, the abdominal muscles, and the respiratory diaphragm. All muscular activity of the body is under the guidance of the nervous system, e.g., contraction of individual cells, isotonic (with normal contraction) or isometric (without normal contraction) exercise, agonist or antagonist activity, and concentric shortening or eccentric lengthening. Breathing is special in that it involves both the somatic nervous system and the autonomic nervous system, the ANS. In other words, you can voluntarily control breathing, or if you choose not to do so, the body automatically takes over. Both systems are connected. The ANS is self-regulating and usually not controlled by the somatic nervous system. For example, you cannot voluntarily decide to speed up or slow down your heart rate. This is normally regulated by the ANS and is beyond control of the somatic nervous system. However, you can influence the heart rate by consciously regulating the respiratory rate because breathing connects both nervous systems. *Long exhalations slow down the heart rate.*

So, by modulating our respiratory rate at will, we influence the ANS. Therefore, breathing offers an important gateway into the world of the ANS. This is important because in advanced Adrenal Fatigue Syndrome, the autonomic nervous system is invariably dysfunctional.

Remember from earlier discussions that the ANS is broadly divided:

1. Into the sympathetic nervous system (SNS), which is responsible for adrenaline release and the fight-or-flight response; and

2. The parasympathetic nervous system (PNS), which is responsible for rest and relaxation of the body's internal functions.

We need less air in quiet times, and the PNS mildly constricts the smooth muscle that surrounds the airways. However, in times of emergency or increased physical activity, the SNS opens the airways and allows air to flow more easily.

To modulate and maintain homeostasis in the body's inner world, the PNS, through release of its neurotransmitter, acetylcholine, works in a dynamic balance with the SNS, through release of its neurotransmitter, norepinephrine. Advanced Adrenal Fatigue Syndrome is invariably tied to over-stimulation of the SNS and the AHS. Extensive experiments have compared Type A (aggressive and high strung) with Type B (laid back and relaxed) personalities. They found that during exposure to various laboratory and clinical stressors, Type A individuals have about threefold larger plasma norepinephrine responses and fourfold larger adrenaline responses than Type B individuals. These chemical transmitters flood the body in Type A individuals, which puts the body on constant alert. This leads to a viscous downward spiral of compensatory response and ultimately adrenal burnout.

One key to adrenal recovery is to reduce SNS tone and enhance PNS tone. This is where Adrenal Breathing can help greatly, because it influences the autonomic circuits that slow the heartbeat and reduce blood pressure, producing calm and a sense of stability. Further, it calms the mind, and allows the body's internal homeostatic system to reset itself. Controlled respiration consciously gives us access to autonomic function that no other system of the body can boast.

Those with severe adrenal weakness often exhibit abnormal breathing patterns that can over-stimulate the SNS, which in turn can trigger panic attacks and contribute to adrenal crashes. We tend to breathe shallowly or even hold our breath when we are feeling anxious or under stress, and sometimes we're not aware of it. Shallow breathing also limits oxygen intake and adds further stress to the body, thus creating a vicious cycle. As we'll describe in the instructions for Adrenal Breathing, holding the breath at the end of inhalation or exhalation stimulates the SNS, thus aggravating adrenal weakness if the body is already in a state of low adrenal reserve.

Adrenal Breathing Exercises are so important because they can break this negative cycle by rebalancing the ANS, thereby gently delivering more oxygen to the body to naturally generate energy without over-stimulating the SNS. Proper Adrenal Breathing enhances the PNS, the parasympathetic nervous system's function, and shifts the body's basal resting mode from a sympathetic to a parasympathetic bias.

Bear in mind that in eastern cultures, breathing is also used to stimulate the SNS. We see this in certain types of yoga breathing. Various techniques involve holding the breath with increasing intensity and performing quick breathing exercises with high frequency (bellow breathing).

Another technique, called thoracic or paradoxical breathing, involves using only the chest wall to affect breathing. The chest wall expands while the abdominal wall is drawn inward toward the back during inhalation and outward during exhalation. While these breathing techniques are empowering and increase energy flow, they can drain the body of the already low energy state in Adrenal Fatigue Syndrome as the SNS is already fully activated.

In Adrenal Breathing, the goal is to *reduce* sympathetic tone. Therefore, we recommend restricting all sympathetically driven breathing techniques until the adrenals are healed or unless directed by your healthcare professional.

Other Benefits

After a few weeks of consistent practice, this abdominal breathing technique will automatically lead to stronger diaphragm muscles. You will notice an automatic increase in your inhalation and exhalation capacity with the same effort, often extending to 90 percent or even 95 percent of capacity. This is achieved effortlessly, calmly, being fully relaxed and with no need to force your breath.

Note, too, that the muscles that connect the ribs (intercostal muscles) are passive and not actively engaged during Adrenal Breathing. Therefore, your chest wall expands and contracts naturally as air flows in and out of the lungs, usually with minimal movement. Since no special effort is directed toward the chest wall to help the breathing process, you won't note any significant rise and fall during the Adrenal Breathing process.

When properly done, Adrenal Breathing Exercises use the diaphragm to help restore adrenal health by:

- enhancing parasympathetic tone
- improving lymphatic circulation, thus clearing toxic metabolites
- improving vital capacity
- supporting healthy ANS balance
- improving tissue oxygen saturation
- optimizing musculoskeletal tone
- effecting gentle rhythmic massage on the GI track and internal organs including the adrenals

This is one of the easiest and most effective exercises anyone with Adrenal Fatigue Syndrome can do at anytime and anyplace to support adrenal recovery.

Adrenal Breathing Exercise

Let's begin with the Adrenal Breathing Exercise. Here are step-by-step instructions:

1. Lie down on your back on a flat but comfortable surface, arms and palms facing up and slightly away from the body with legs uncrossed and apart at shoulder width. Loosen your clothes as needed. Make a conscious effort to relax and feel the weight of the body on the floor. You can also do this breathing in a sitting position with your spine straight (do not arch your back because the abdominal muscles wrap around to the rear). Those in advanced AFS and who are weak should begin practicing this exercise in the supine position. As the body strengthens, you can do this exercise in either a sitting or standing position. (If space does not permit the supine position during this breathing exercise, then a sitting or standing position is acceptable.)

2. Close your eyes. (If desired, you can cover your eyes with a small towel.) Drop your tongue to its natural relaxed resting position toward the back of the mouth without obstructing air flow. It is very important to keep your spine straight, drop your shoulders and let them relax. Check yourself for these items before going any further.

3. Exhale completely through your mouth, making a small whoosh sound. Now you are ready to start.

4. Close your mouth and inhale quietly through your nose. Start at 50 percent of capacity in a smooth and rhythmic fashion. (Working yourself up to 80-90 percent of capacity depends on how well you can perform this breathing.) From this point on, don't breathe through the mouth.

5. Imagine the air entering your body through your left nostril, which according to ancient tradition, is calming. Your belly should be expanding outward as you inhale comfortably. If you put your hands on your stomach, they will be pushed away from the back. This ensures that you are breathing properly.

   Imagine you are filling your body with air from the bottom up. Focus your attention on the flow of air in and out of the nasal passages, in through the left and out through the right nostril. Breathe evenly, and do not force the breath.

   During this breathing exercise, the chest wall does not move significantly, but the abdominal muscles must be completely free and relaxed. (If they are even mildly tensed you can't do the breathing correctly.) The rest of the body is stable except for a slight backward movement of the head during inhalation. Don't forget that eyes are closed, with shoulders dropped and relaxed throughout.

6. Do a mental count of four slowly and comfortably (about 1-2 seconds per count). At the end of the inhalation, spontaneously progress to exhale naturally and without effort. Inhalation can occur only as a result of

muscular activity; however, exhalations are different, as the lungs have the capacity to get smaller because their elasticity keeps pulling them, along with the rib cage, to a smaller size.

Do not hold your breath intentionally at the end of inhalation or exhalation. What we want from relaxed, even breathing is a smooth rhythmic transition from inhalation to exhalation and from exhalation to inhalation—no jerky movements.

The actual pattern of breathing is elliptical rather than circular. Even though no air is moving in or out at the ends of inhalation and exhalation, you can smoothly merge inhalation with exhalation (and exhalation with inhalation) without effort if you focus on rhythmic movement along the ellipse.

7. Exhale completely through your nose, while imagining the air coming out of the right nostril, quietly and smoothly. There is no count required on exhalation. Feel your stomach contract slowly until most (but not all) of the air is out naturally. Exhalation is normally a little longer than inhalation. Do not force, overextend, or hold after the exhalation, because that will activate the SNS. Simply let the body control the exhalation time and intensity naturally.

   This is one full breath. Now inhale again and repeat the cycle seven more times for a total of eight full breaths. A full set is eight complete breaths, which takes most people 1-2 minutes.

It's important to do at least one set of eight full breaths each time you start Adrenal Breathing. Let's examine why.

When you first maintain a stationary position that is comfortable, especially in a flat position with face up (supine), most of the motor neurons that innervate the skeletal muscles are still firing nerve impulses automatically. With each breath, however, the number and frequency of nerve impulses transmitted to your muscles starts to decline. This is an automatic physiological response of Adrenal Breathing. With practice, within a minute or two (1-2 sets of 8 breaths each), the number of nerve impulses to the muscles of your hands and toes is drastically reduced and relaxation increases. Within five minutes (3-4 sets of breathing), the motor neuronal input to the muscles of your limbs diminishes and approaches zero if you are in a supine position. This effect, along with the rhythmical movement of the respiratory diaphragm, draws you into even deeper relaxation with full activation of the PNS. The mind and body is fully connected and engaged.

Immediately following the Adrenal Breathing Exercise, most individuals report a sense of calm, peace, reduced fatigue, and renewed sense of "being," a result of the mind-body connection. However, although it seems paradoxical, any *drastic* improvement in energy immediately after the exercise indicates over-exertion. Similarly, if you feel lightheaded or agitated when you first breathe this way, reduce frequency or intensity until you feel comfortable and relaxed during the entire exercise.

The key to success is persistency and consistency. Most people start reporting benefits within a few days, but it can take up to 20 or more days, depending on the degree of Adrenal Fatigue Syndrome and ANS dysfunction. Those who have a high sympathetic overtone bias or bad breathing habits will take longer to see results.

Adrenal Breathing uses basic techniques of abdominal breathing, or belly breathing, because this is where movement can be seen and felt. During inhalation, the belly expands and moves away from the back of the body toward the front (anterior). During exhalation, the opposite happens and the belly contracts and moves toward the back of the body (posterior). What makes Adrenal Breathing unique is the focus on intensity that is matched to the body's capacity.

Caution: Follow the above instructions; start slowly and work your way up. Start with 50 percent breath intensity and increase to 80 percent as tolerated.

These exercises are much more powerful than they appear, and if you're in advanced AFS (e.g., Stages 3C and 3D) you may not be able to tolerate them when you first try. Immediately reduce the intensity of each breath if you experience shortness of breath, increased pulse rate, strengthening heartbeat, or fatigue, and reduce the length of each session accordingly. Make sure you're not taking too many breaths per set, and do not hold your breath at the end of inhalation or exhalation. You should feel good after each session, not worse. Always listen to your body, and remember that overzealous breathing may trigger an adrenal crash.

Tip: Adrenal Breathing Exercises can help you relax before you go to sleep for the night, or fall back to sleep if you awaken in the middle of the night. If you cannot fall asleep, do not simply lie in bed and fret about not sleeping or passively feel the time go by. Instead, do a few sets of Adrenal Breathing Exercises.

Recommended Protocol

- **Day 1-3:** Start by doing one set (8 breaths) twice a day, once upon awakening and before breakfast and again at bedtime right before going to sleep. The sessions should take 1-2 minutes each.
- **Day 4-6:** Increase to one set five times a day: on awakening, midmorning (10-11AM), early afternoon (1-2 PM), late afternoon (4-5 PM), and at night before going to sleep.
- **Day 7-9:** Continue five times a day, but *increase from one set to two sets* each session (16 complete breaths). This should take 2-3 minutes per session.
- **Day 10-12:** Continue five times a day, but *increase from two sets to three sets* each session (24 complete breaths). This should take 3-4 minutes each session.
- **Day 13 onwards:** If you feel up to it, continue five sessions a day, but *increase from three sets to five sets* each time (40 complete breaths). This will take about 5-6 minutes per session. If you do not feel well with this intensity, decrease back down to three sets per session, but keep the five sessions a day unchanged.

Consider the protocol a general recommendation only. Those in severe Adrenal Fatigue Syndrome may not be able to progress as recommended and in fact, can get worse if they progress too quickly. Always seek professional guidance prior to beginning. A detailed audio CD on Adrenal Breathing is available from *DrLam.com.*

While you cannot overdo Adrenal Breathing, we recommend that you do not exceed five sets of breathing exercises each session and no more than five sessions a day without consulting your healthcare professional. Once you practice Adrenal Breathing, you could be ready to proceed to the more advanced adrenal stretches and restorative and rebuilding exercises to speed up your recovery process.

Advanced Adrenal Breathing Exercises

After mastering basic Adrenal Breathing, those wishing to expand the breathing capacity further may engage in mild contraction of the lower thoracic muscles during exhalation to further close the chest wall and expel the air. Mild backward contraction of the scapulas (flat bones in the back) during inhalation will also help to open the chest wall. The body remains relaxed during the entire process.

Advanced breathing using both abdominal and thoracic muscle will activate both the PNS and ANS. Because of the stimulatory component, advanced Adrenal Breathing is a good auxiliary form of strengthening the adrenal glands *only* if used at the right time. Overzealous self-navigation programs or inexperienced clinicians can use this breathing incorrectly and worsen AFS, triggering adrenal crashes.

Adrenal Restorative Exercise (ARE)

A complete Adrenal Fatigue Syndrome recovery program must incorporate techniques and exercises designed to restore the health and balance of the nervous system. Adrenal Restorative Exercise (ARE) is a set of specially designed exercises that promote deep and active relaxation. These exercises adapt established restorative yoga poses to enhance adrenal function; they focus on a key aspect of Adrenal Fatigue Syndrome, repairing the mind-body connection and restoring nervous system homeostasis.

ARE is unlike regular exercise, which directs you to focus on stretching and strengthening. For those in Adrenal Fatigue Syndrome, the regular approach leaves sufferers feeling physically strained and exhausted, and in some people this triggers adrenal crash. On the other hand, ARE is designed to help those people with Adrenal Fatigue Syndrome, for whom even gentle stretching is too active and for whom a priority is the need to restore their health and regain balance in their lives. Those with injuries, recent surgery, or prolonged and chronic physical conditions, such as high blood pressure, will find ARE a breakthrough experience.

Adrenal Restorative Exercise focuses on being—connecting the mind and body—thereby allowing signals from the mind and body to reconnect in a restorative and nurturing mode. These exercises rely on a customized sequence of specially designed postures in which your body is comfortably supported. This allows your joints to open and the muscles to relax and melt into place instead of stretching and straining into position. Blood flow to the adrenals is increased, and the nervous system switches to a calm state and a mode that promotes deep inner healing.

The Essence of Adrenal Restorative Exercise

- Promotes activation of the parasympathetic nervous system (PNS) without over-stimulating the sympathetic nervous system (SNS) or the adrenomedullary hormonal system (AHS).
- Promotes joint motility and range of motion to overcome the immobility that is common in Adrenal Fatigue Syndrome.
- Improves postures and biomechanics of the body function.

- Allows muscles to relax without worsening the catabolic (breakdown) state.
- Enhances blood flow to the adrenal glands to support recovery.

What you need and what to do:

Equipment: Soft support such as a towel, pillow, cushion, chair, or sofa. If a cushion is uncomfortable, then use a folded towel adjusted to a comfortable height. A yoga bolster is not required but is useful if your body is flexible.

Environment: A quiet room, free of distraction and noise. Clothing should be loose and not constrictive at the waist or over the rest of the body.

Breathing Technique: Use only Adrenal Breathing throughout the session. Take full breaths up to 80-90 percent of vital capacity, using the diaphragm only, with smooth, regular, rhythmic nasal breathing, imagining the air coming in through the left nostril and going out through the right nostril. Do not force any breath.

Duration: This program consists of 12 sequential positions or poses that you assume for one minute per pose for poses 1-11, and three minutes for pose number 12. The entire session takes about 15 minutes but can be as long as one hour simply by proportionately extending the amount of time spent in each pose. Beginners may start with as little as 20 seconds per pose and slowly increase the time.

Protocol: The protocol is divided into four parts, with three poses per part. It is best to perform the exercise in sequence, from 1-12.

Note: Adrenal Restorative Exercise can be too simulating for those with advanced Adrenal Fatigue Syndrome, especially during an adrenal crash. Do not start this protocol unless recommended by your healthcare professional. Stop at any point you have a sense of the body becoming overexcited, anxious, or jittery, and report the experience to your healthcare professional.

Part 1: Neck Restorative Sequence

We start ARE with relaxing the neck. The neck represents the anatomical area of the body that is critical in the overall nervous system, because this is where the major nerves and arteries branch off. Your neck muscles and your posture control the spine and set the muscular tone for the rest of your body to follow. You cannot have a relaxed body if your neck is tense. Conversely, the body cannot help but relax once the neck muscles are rested.

Pose 1: Half Lotus:

This pose focuses on neck relaxation, breathing, and calming of the body.

Sit on the floor comfortably, with your legs crossed in half lotus position (left foot touching the right inner thigh or vice versa, as you are able to perform). Beginners will find comfort by sitting on some form of support (folded towel, pillow, or cushion) to prop up the hips just a bit.

Make sure the spine is straight.

Your hands are comfortably extended in front of you, with the elbows resting on the inner part of the hips or thighs. Palms are facing up.

To ensure that the neck muscles are not tense, relax and drop your shoulders. Head is straight, eyes closed. Tongue is dropped backwards.

Start Adrenal Breathing.

Tip: For maximum restorative effect, place extra support on the outside part of each knee.

Tip: If you find it difficult to sit on the floor with legs crossed, sit on a chair with your feet resting on a stool if possible. Do not cross your feet.

Pose 2: Half Lotus Variation:

This pose focuses on neck and shoulder muscle relaxation.

While in half lotus position (pose 1), drop your head forward with eyes looking at the belly button. Now close your eyes. The back remains straight, shoulders are dropped.

Experience total relaxation of the neck as the head comfortably rests in its natural flexed position. Tongue is dropped backwards. Eyes remain closed.

Start Adrenal Breathing.

Tip: If you are doing this while sitting on a chair, place a cushion on a table and rest your forehead on the support.

Pose 3: Child Pose:

This pose focuses on relaxation of the neck, shoulder, and upper limbs.

Remain on the floor (or in the chair).

Spread the knees as wide as is comfortable,
keeping the big toes touching, with knees flexed.
The back of your thigh is now resting on your calf muscles.

Bring the belly to rest between the thighs, with the forehead to the floor.

Bring the arms alongside the thighs with the palms facing upwards.
Experience the total relaxation of neck, shoulders, and upper limbs.
Shoulders are dropped. The back is still straight but not stiff.
Tongue is dropped backwards. Close your eyes.

Start Adrenal Breathing.

Tip: For extra restorative effect, place support underneath your knees, between your thighs, and under your forehead.

Part 2: Spine Restorative Sequence

The next three poses are designed to open up the spine and properly realign body posture. This is important because all key muscles in the body are connected to the spine directly or indirectly. Proper spinal alignment controls muscles, and therefore, the vessels and nerves that run through it.

Pose 4: Supported Fish Pose:

This pose focuses on expanding the chest wall.

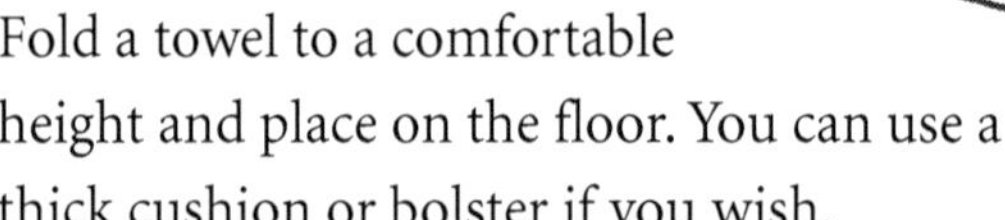

Fold a towel to a comfortable height and place on the floor. You can use a thick cushion or bolster if you wish.

Lie down (supine), face up, with the upper back resting on the support.
Feet are at shoulder width, arms along the side of the body, palms up.

To support the neck, place a rolled up towel underneath the neck.

Tilt your head back, with the chin facing upwards toward the sky. The neck is hyper-extended but comfortable.

Feel how the chest wall opens up, and your lung capacity is increased.

The body is now totally relaxed. Shoulders are down. Tongue is back.

Close your eyes.

Start Adrenal Breathing.

Tip: For extra restorative effect, place support beneath both knees and neck.

Pose 5: Supported Lumbar Expansion:

This pose focuses on expanding the lower back and the pelvis.

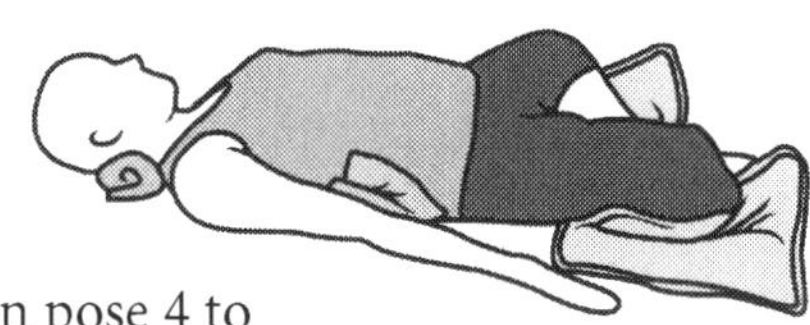

Move the support used in pose 4 to the lower back (lumbar) area. Head returns to normal position and resting comfortably on the floor, with a towel behind the neck for support as needed. Do not tilt the head.

Flex both knees, bringing the feet together, with the bottom of each foot touching the other if possible. Note how the pelvis is opening up. Tongue is back, shoulders are down, and all limbs are in a comfortable position. Close your eyes.

Start Adrenal Breathing.

Tip: For extra restorative effect, place support on the outside of each knee.

Pose 6: Supported Full Spine Expansion:

This pose focuses on the entire spine, with upper back and lower back simultaneously expanded.

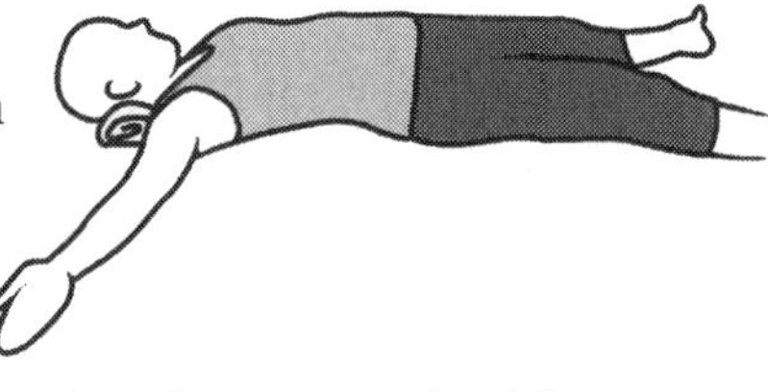

Roll your towel(s) the long way, enough to reach from the shoulders to the tail bone. Lay your back over the towel, so the towel is under your entire spine. Support neck with a folded hand towel.

Open your legs to a position about shoulder width apart. Arms are extended to the side, horizontal to shoulder, with palms up. You look like a starfish.

Experience the entire back curving around the raised towel from left to right. The chest wall and lumbar areas are expanded. Tongue is back, shoulders are down.

Start Adrenal Breathing.

Tip: Place your arms next to you if you find a horizontal position uncomfortable.

Part 3: Circulation Restorative Sequence

Now that the neck and shoulder muscles are relaxed (poses 1-3) and the spine is opened (poses 4-6), we are ready to restore the body's circulation to maximum flow, while removing any strain on tissues that may interfere with this process. We accomplish this by opening the two key outlets where circulation flows: the thoracic outlet and the femoral outlet.

Pose 7: Supported Bent Knee:

This pose focuses on increasing the circulation to the head.

Lie supine on the floor, with knees bent and feet resting comfortably on a sofa or chair. (A support for the lower back often helps.)

Place your arms alongside the body, palms up. The back lumbar area is resting on the floor and free of tension. Tongue is back, shoulders are down. Eyes are closed.

Start Adrenal Breathing.

Pose 8: Diagonal Thoracic and Femoral Outlet Expansion:

While in supine position with pose 7, lift and bend your left knee and place the left foot comfortably on the right thigh.

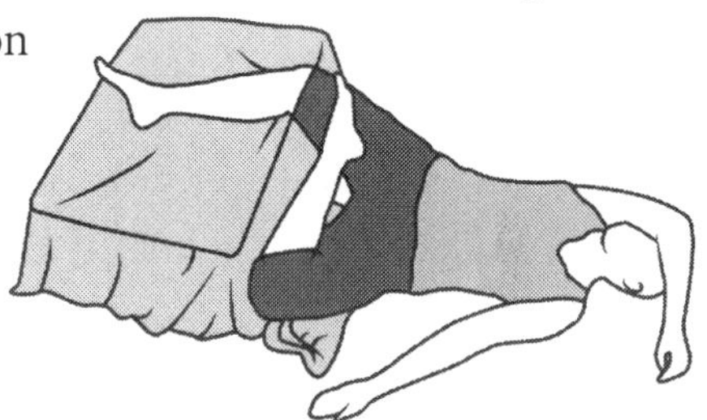

Let the left knee drop comfortably (as you can tolerate). Use extra support to prop up the bent knee. This relaxes any connective tissue impingement around the groin area (inguinal) and opens up the femoral artery, allowing maximum blood flow to the lower extremities.

Now raise your right arm, and place it over your face without impeding your breathing. The inside part of the elbow should be resting comfortably on the forehead, with palm facing down, and the forearm resting in a comfortable position. This opens up the thoracic outlet. You can actually feel the softness in the lower mid-clavicle space, that is, the area on either side of the neck. Use support to prop up any uncomfortable area(s).

Tongue is back, shoulders are down. Eyes are closed.

Start Adrenal Breathing.

Pose 9: Reverse of Pose 8: Repeat the sequence using the right knee and arm.

Part 4: Mind-Body Restoration Sequence

With the neck and shoulders relaxed, the spine opened, and blood flow optimized, we come to the final sequence designed to connect the mind and body. All previous poses are designed to prepare the body for this mind-body reconnection.

Pose 10: Supported Fetal Left: This pose focuses on the body's calm state of being. A calm mind helps us to direct our body energy toward healing to balance the nervous system and the adrenal glands.

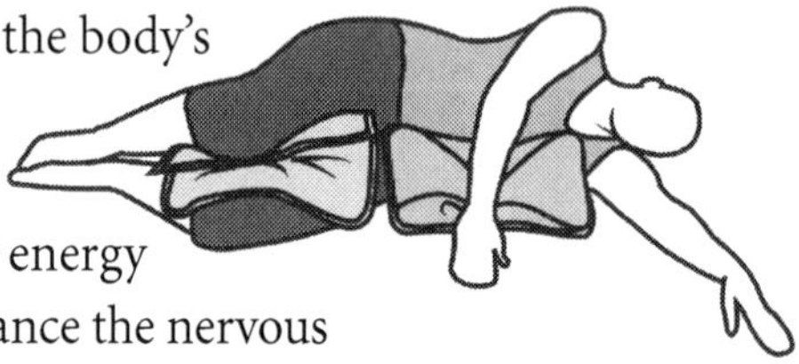

Place support on the floor and lie down on your left side in a fetal position, with the left side of the body on the support. The degree of support can vary depending on the person. Bolsters are excellent tools. Place additional support like a pillow between your knees.

Both arms are in a comfortable position. Head is supported. Abdominal wall is unimpeded. Tongue is back, shoulders are down. Eyes are closed.

Start Adrenal Breathing.

Pose 11: Supported Fetal Right: Repeat Pose 10 on your right side.

Pose 12: Deep Relaxation (In traditional yoga, this is also called Savasana or Corpse Pose): This is the last and most important of all 12 restorative exercises. It is also the most difficult pose to do well, but the most vital to perform correctly. This exercise promotes total body calm.

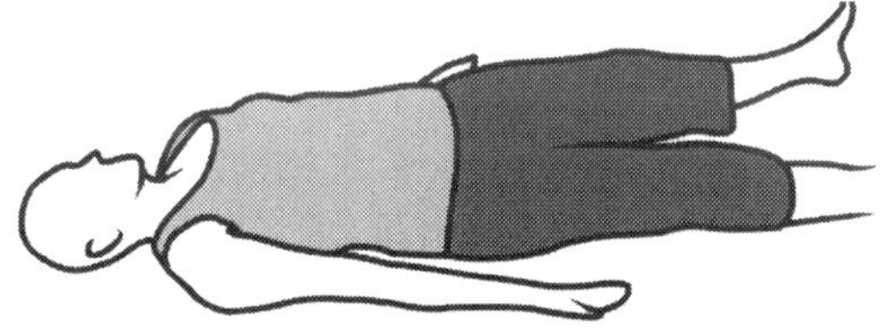

Lie down on the back, letting the feet fall out to either side. Bring the arms alongside, but slightly separated from the body, palms facing up. Relax the whole body, including the face. Let the body feel heavy.

The position of the head is crucial. Keep your chin even with the forehead or slightly lower, which is a relaxed position. (When the head is tilted back, the position is stimulating and, therefore, undesirable.) The tongue is back, shoulders are down, and the eyes are closed.

Start Adrenal Breathing.

To come out, first begin to deepen the breath, and
then awaken the body by moving your fingers and toes.

Bring the knees into the chest. Turn to the right side and slowly sit up. (Do not abruptly rise from a supine to a standing position as this may lead to dizziness.)

Note: Stay in this position three times longer than all other poses. For example, if you stay one minute per pose from pose 1-11, then stay 3 minutes for pose 12.

Adrenal Yoga Exercise

Some individuals mistakenly believe that yoga is a religion, but though it developed centuries ago in India, it is not a form of Hinduism. Modern yoga dates back to the late nineteenth century, and today, Christians, Buddhists, Jews, Muslims, and many other groups, even agnostics and atheists, happily practice yoga. Certainly, a spiritual side to yoga exists, but we don't need to subscribe to any particular belief to benefit. Those without a particular religious bent often speak of the inner or human spirit or the highest self, concepts that affirm the value of life.

We recommend yoga for AFS because it is a systematic technology to improve the body, understand the mind, and free the spirit. Overall, yoga practitioners tend to be more flexible, stronger, more energetic, thinner, and more youthful than others, and all these attributes are welcome and desirable in Adrenal Fatigue Syndrome recovery.

Yoga practice leads to strengthening and calming the nervous system, thereby balancing the dysfunctional stress-response system we see in AFS sufferers. Blood flow to internal organs is increased, and the body delivers more oxygen to the adrenal glands, which promotes healing. Equally important, yoga practice helps clear mental clutter—mind chatter—that interferes with finding clarity and even helps in listening to the voices of intuition and creativity.

Yoga practice cultivates spiritual and physical muscles, which over time, leads to greater happiness, less anxiety, and greater peace. Because yoga builds on itself, it becomes more effective over time. It is equivalent to learning how to play a musical instrument: The longer you stick with it and practice, the better you become and the more benefits you reap.

Adrenal Yoga takes the best of *traditional* yoga and modifies it to suit those with Adrenal Fatigue Syndrome. For example, certain stretching and strengthening exercises known as asanas are removed, because they can stimulate the SNS, along with certain breathing techniques known as pranayama that can trigger a release of adrenaline. On the other hand, posture and lung capacity are improved as are bowel function, lymphatic draining, and the function of the immune system.

Gradually, one feels more balanced and the body is better able to endure the inevitable stress of daily living. Therefore, Adrenal Yoga is about restoring internal balance, and with balance, internal control. It is not about physical flexibility. We see many individuals with Adrenal Fatigue Syndrome who are already quite flexible. It is not about increasing strength, as many men and women are strong and still suffer from Adrenal Fatigue Syndrome. Adrenal Yoga enables us to transform liabilities such as fear, inability to relax, low energy, anxiety, and depression into strength, giving the person more control and a more balanced feeling. Here are the levels of Adrenal Yoga:

- Beginning Adrenal Yoga focuses on breathing and stretching. This forms the foundation of internal control.

- Intermediate Adrenal Yoga focuses on strength and toning. This serves to reverse the catabolic state and stabilize metabolic function.
- Adrenal Yoga focuses on fluidity and control. This serves to fine tune internal body homeostasis.

Note: Adrenal Yoga consists of 21 sessions and is available on DVD at *www.DrLam.com.*

Regular Yoga

When you are ready to do yoga in a commercial yoga studio, health club, gym or local Y, or you choose to follow a DVD at home, remember that you are still recovering from AFS and, as such, building your reserves. We recommend choosing a level of yoga that challenges you and goes beyond what you have accomplished with Adrenal Yoga. However, we've observed a tendency to be overly aggressive, and even with yoga, this kind of pushing can trigger adrenal crash. Whether you are practicing yoga at home or in an outside setting, the following tips may help you avoid any backlash or injury:

- In your poses, find an edge for yourself where you are challenged but not overwhelmed. At this edge, practice maintaining a clear, open, and accepting mental state.
- Give yourself permission to rest when you feel overworked.
- Pay close attention to what you are saying to yourself as you practice, and make an intentional effort to appreciate your own efforts and innate goodness.
- Faithfully go to class or practice at home. If you practice outside your home, arrive at the class early to give yourself time to talk to others in the class.

- Realize that the development of qualities like patience, discipline, wisdom, right effort, kindness, gratitude, and many others will arise from your yoga practice. These qualities create a steady and soft mind.
- Find a teacher who offers a balance of gentleness and firmness and whose teaching inspires you to practice from your highest self.

Recognize that simply attending class is a major statement of courage, self-care, and positive momentum. Realize that you are inspiring others as you become truer to your deepest desires.

Power Yoga

Power yoga represents an advanced form of yoga that focuses on the core strength. Power yoga is a general term used in the West to describe a vigorous, fitness-based approach to yoga, generally modeled on the Ashtanga practice style. The term *power yoga* came into common usage in the mid 1990s, when several yoga teachers sought ways to make Ashtanga yoga more accessible to western students. However, unlike Ashtanga, power yoga does not follow a set series of poses. Therefore, power yoga classes can vary widely from one to the next, but what they share is their emphasis on strength and flexibility.

Power yoga heralded the current popularity of yoga in the U.S. and brought it to studios and gyms all over the country, especially because so many individuals began to see yoga as a way to work out. Back in the 1950s and '60s, gentler forms of yoga became popular in the U.S., which gradually led to its wide availability. Power yoga has its greatest appeal among those who are already quite fit and enjoy exercise. With consistent practice, muscle definition becomes prominent, toning is enhanced, and strength is improved.

Another Component: Aerobics

As you probably know, aerobic exercise includes long duration and slow paced activities such as walking, slow jogging, rowing, cycling (including slow cycling), and any other form of exercise that involves endurance. This type of exercise will help decrease cortisol levels and aid in burning body fat as well. Aerobic exercise benefits those who have stressed adrenal glands in the early stages, where cortisol output is high. However, keep in mind the following principles:

- Intense aerobic exercise can also worsen adrenal function. Those with advanced adrenal weakness should not consider any activities more strenuous than walking (or exercise recommended by their healthcare provider). Excessive aerobic activities drain the body of already low energy reserves.
- We recommend that those in advanced Adrenal Fatigue Syndrome avoid all aerobic activities other than walking. Frequency and duration varies from person to person. Some in advanced stages might be able to tolerate only five minutes of walking every other day.
- We generally introduce aerobic exercise carefully and slowly as recovery returns to Stage 3B. Then, as Adrenal Fatigue Syndrome improves to Stage 3A and later Stage 2, the frequency and intensity can be increased.

As you can see, we consider it a goal in AFS recovery to return to exercise and develop the mind and body from the core through a series of systematic gentle exercises. Those who take these exercises seriously will be happy to know that many have gone from a bedridden state to running long distance races within a short time after starting with us, and an important tool used in their recovery and training were the exercises we mention and describe here. Exercise is part of what we know as, and consider to be, "regular" life.

Relationships also are a component of normal life, but relationships can be stressful, too. In the next chapter, we talk about the way relationships can interfere with AFS recovery.

Key Points to Remember

- Exercise is an important tool for AFS recovery, but it has to be done right. Engaging in the wrong exercise regimen can often trigger adrenal crashes.
- Those with advanced AFS must be careful in exercise progression, starting with Adrenal Breathing Exercise, progressing to Adrenal Restorative Exercise, and then ending with Adrenal Yoga Exercise.
- When properly done, one should not feel drained after exercise.
- Most of us do not sufficiently appreciate the healing power of breathing. Adrenal breathing is the most important exercise for many in advanced stages. This is different from other types of exercise in that it helps to lower sympathetic tone while enhancing parasympathetic response.
- Aerobics and power yoga exercise can be added to the overall exercise program as AFS recovery proceeds.

Chapter 6

Your Relationships Influence Adrenal Fatigue Syndrome

Earlier, we discussed the mind-body connection, and now that you understand more about it, and about Adrenal Fatigue Syndrome, you likely can see how important the mind is in maintaining and enjoying good health. In the past, this has often been overlooked. Neuroscience research has now proven beyond a doubt that the mind and the body are connected. Nothing affects the mind more than our relationships, because unpleasant or dysfunctional relationships cause enormous emotional stress.

Chronic stress is the leading cause of Adrenal Fatigue Syndrome, and as you know, stressors come in all shapes and sizes, so to speak, including physical, emotional, or financial. Those who regularly physically over-exert, such as serious professional or even amateur athletes, are at high risk of developing AFS. However, as athletes learn through experience, the effects of physical stress can usually be reversed and the body nurtured back to health with rest and other measures. Other stressors, such as overwork, poor diet, and overexertion, usually act as underlying triggers of adrenal crashes. However, we've also noted that in and of itself, financial distress is seldom the root stressor cause of AFS.

Emotional and mental stress and distress represent the most common stressors that contribute to AFS. Issues related to unresolved toxic relationships usually cause such stress because they gradually wear our bodies down over time. We have found it truly amazing how much your emotional health can influence your physical health. As we've said, advanced AFS can be considered a mind-body disorder in its broadest sense. A strong mind-body connection is a powerful healing force we can harness to improve and maintain health. However, on the flipside, as in Adrenal Fatigue Syndrome, the mind-body connection can also have a devastating negative force that's capable of ruining your body.

Those who are in advanced AFS will tell you how easy it is to have an adrenal crash after a heated debate or an unpleasant encounter, especially if it is with someone close to you. Your adrenaline starts pumping, anxiety sets in, heart rate goes up, force of heart beat goes up, you become drained, and quickly become bedridden. Clearly, maintaining a good relationship with those around you is conducive to the healing process.

Numerous studies support the belief that individuals with an upbeat and positive perspective tend to be healthier and enjoy longer lives than those who take a gloomy and cynical attitude about the future. We now see an emerging influence factor, *epigeneticism*, which contends that environmental factors such as diet and stress influence the expression of your genes.

Remember that the *expression* of your genes, not the genes themselves, dictate whether you develop certain diseases. For example, if you have *constitutionally* weak adrenal glands, stress may cause this weakness to be expressed, which then leads to Adrenal Fatigue Syndrome. On the other hand, the absence of stress can delay the expression of this weakness for an indefinite period.

As you age, your genes do not change, but your epigenome changes dramatically. It is influenced by how you react to physical and emotional stresses. Virtually everything that happens in your environment, from something as amorphous as climate change to something as specific as marriage, ultimately affects your epigenome. Everyday issues such as the building up to taking final exams or the lingering effects of childhood abuse, also influence your epigenome.

Relationships and Well-being

Relationships also influence the expression of your genes and have a direct impact on your tendency to either avoid or develop unpleasant conditions, from heart palpitations to Adrenal Fatigue Syndrome to depression. For example, studies have shown:

- Heart surgery patients with strong spiritual and social support have a mortality rate 1/7th of those who do not have these advantages.
- Meditating for just 30 minutes a day can be as effective as the use of antidepressants.
- Elderly people with positive attitudes have an over 20 percent reduction in risk of death from cardiovascular disease and over 50 percent lower risk of death from all other causes.

We can clearly see that the ability to build positive mental attitudes greatly affects your physical health, and this applies to Adrenal Fatigue Syndrome. In fact, if emotional stressors are present but not resolved, they impede recovery.

It can be liberating to know that the ability to manifest positive emotions and happiness is perhaps one of our greatest human characteristics. You needn't feel bad because you're getting older or are tired much of the time, or because your life isn't going exactly as you had planned. Once you make your mind up to be happy, you really don't have to feel bad for any reason at all. In addition, if you view it from a positive perspective, AFS might turn out to be one of the best things that has happened to you.

A Wakeup Call

For many, AFS serves as a much needed wakeup call, signaling that one or more areas of life are out of balance or misaligned. Addressing Adrenal Fatigue Syndrome often becomes the starting point for an exploration of life at a deeper level. For some, this involves recognizing the role of toxic relationships.

Day to day, most of us tend to live superficially, and we may need a significant wakeup call, such as AFS, to nudge us to live at a much deeper level. This often involves understanding the body and mind from a spiritual perspective, perhaps relearning and focusing on what we once knew about the truly important things in life—inner peace, love, forgiveness, contentment, and so forth.

No matter how tempting to believe otherwise, Adrenal Fatigue Syndrome, or any serious condition, can't merely be dismissed or handled with a quick fix. If you try for a fast and easy path, you not only fail, you also likely miss the great blessings of self evaluation and the rewards waiting for you when you take the time to reorder your life. We always recommend using AFS as a tool to learn to really listen to and get to know your body, along with rediscovering the broader meaning of your life.

Gaining insight into ourselves and our healing process also means cultivating subtle changes in our thinking and attitudes. For example, we need to transform superficial concerns that focus on negative thinking and feeling like a victim to attitudes that value serenity and peace, no matter how painful the circumstances of the moment. Bear in mind that having a positive attitude is not about being happy all the time, and part of being happy involves accepting that you'll feel down at times.

Although we already have the full potential to be happy, and we control our capacity for happiness, most of us find it extremely difficult. At any given time, the majority of people are unhappy with one thing or another in their lives, from their homes to their jobs to their incomes. However, of all possible challenges and concerns, relationship difficulties remain the most difficult to overcome.

A Barrier to Healing

In the process of examining your life, it's also essential to develop the willingness and strength to let go of toxic and harmful relationships. Again and again, we've seen that AFS patients must heal the mind before the body can fully heal, because the mind controls the body. If we carry emotional baggage, we need to discard it and lighten our emotional load. Since much emotional baggage results from difficult relationships, we need to address them. If we don't, we won't see the mind-body healing we desire.

Of course, at some point, our important long-term relationships, including marriage, family, and close friendships, encounter rough patches involving disagreements and disappointments. Deepening relationship bonds during difficult times and growing through the experience is a hallmark of emotional maturity.

On the other hand, we must face that some relationships are just plain toxic. No matter how we try to work through troubles, conflict and friction poison the well and we and the other person continue to be hurt, and at least one person ends up in an emotional desert.

To be in a toxic relationship doesn't necessarily mean that the individuals involved are bad. Rather, it's more likely that the individuals are a bad fit, and goodness or badness isn't the issue. When personal styles clash, a toxic relationship often develops. Perhaps good chemistry existed at one point, but over time, and perhaps because important events intervened, the people involved changed, thus altering the relationship. This is all part of the human experience. Still, although no one is to blame, the relationship is toxic all the same.

Relationships you consider toxic put your emotional health at risk. Perhaps the other people involved have short tempers, mood swings, inconsistent behavior, or are impulsive and in denial about their behavior. Or, they might admit to behaving badly, but then never try to correct their ways. Sometimes, this kind of toxic relationship can be quite abusive, even if the bad behavior is limited to thoughtless or hostile words. At times, one partner may show only shallow feelings for the other person, or they refuse to engage in meaningful discussion, but instead, threaten to break off the relationship. Some individuals withdraw and withhold their concern and love, leaving the others feeling left out in the cold.

Overall, a person who is toxic to you no longer cares about the marriage, partnership, or friendship and for various reasons remains self-centered. Typically, toxic individuals manipulate their companions and situations to keep a one-up-one-down, dependent relationship and use shame, insult, and sarcasm as weapons against others. Then they look down on the very people they're abusing; this kind of treatment of other people is emotionally abusive and far more common than we may realize.

If you're in the midst of a toxic relationship, isn't it true that you have found yourself chronically tired and angry, and perhaps even frightened? You might constantly be nervous about finding a safe or unsafe time to talk to your partner, or you may question your right to express yourself.

All abusive relationships are by definition toxic. Unfortunately, many individuals stay in these relationships because they have forgotten their rights and options. This kind of low self-esteem can come from depression, fear of loneliness, or harmful threats from an abusive partner. Some probably no longer believe that their lives could improve if they left the toxic relationship behind.

Sadly, marriages and long term partnerships can become abusive over time. It seems that suddenly, the relationship has deteriorated. Some individuals become subtly conditioned to being badly treated, and may forget that the behavior going on in their relationships and home is truly abusive. However, danger signs invariably appear. Here are some important signs to watch for and consider.

Your partner:

- separates you from your family, friends, and children;
- keeps watch over you;
- publically or privately verbally abuses you;
- dominates you and the entire household, not leaving space for your desires and preferences;
- blames you for ruining the relationship and tries to make you change to make things work; and/or
- controls you by being overly possessive and overpowering.

Meanwhile, you:

- begin to believe your own thoughts, words, opinions, and accomplishments have little or no value anymore;
- lose your individual self identity as you depend more on your partner, and you may no longer have confidence that you can survive without him/her;
- become afraid to tell the truth for fear of upsetting your partner; and/or
- find your self esteem has plummeted to a low level as you absorb your partner's abusive remarks meant to make you feel worthless and unattractive.

Emotions and Toxic Relationships

Some specific emotions help people evaluate their relationships. In addition, these feelings may sneak up, so to speak, and only when they see a list or someone asks pointed questions do they suddenly say, "Hey, that's me. That's how I feel much of the time." Like AFS itself, this realization is its own wakeup call. Consider if any of the following currently relate to you:

- Unsupported
- Dissatisfied
- Fearful
- Exasperated
- Depleted/Drained
- Unaccepted/Unrewarded
- Judged
- Guilty

- Tired
- Angry
- Untrusting
- Unequal
- Stifled
- Shamed
- Stressed

Recognizing a Toxic Relationship Cycle

Most of us want to find love and intimacy, but we're also afraid of being hurt; we worry about making a commitment, but we dread abandonment. The feelings around commitment and fear of abandonment are also known as anxiety. The relationship comfort zone is flanked by highly individual behavior patterns, which are not close enough to trigger *fusion anxiety*, nor too distant to trigger separation *anxiety*. We formed these boundaries in our childhood and unless we bring them into the realm of our conscious awareness we seldom change. Our boundaries are capable of creating positive patterns, of course, but they also create patterns that can lead to a toxic relationship cycle.

In a toxic relationship cycle, power struggles arise again and again, but no solutions are found. Intimacy turns into conflict, which then leads to anxiety, often triggering fear of loss. These anxieties and fears trigger arguments that end with hurt feelings and withdrawal. Though withdrawal might bring temporary relief, it ultimately turns into feelings of isolation and loneliness, thus setting off anxieties about abandonment. We often see this separation anxiety leading to new declarations and proposals, which renew intimacy; the couple (even couples involved in truly abusive relationships) goes through a *honeymoon* period. However, this closeness soon triggers fusion anxiety and trouble starts all over again, thus initiating another repetition of cyclical behavior.

In terms of AFS, each time the cycle occurs, the adrenals take another beating. With each stress, the adrenal glands increase their demand for cortisol. With time, this output eventually declines, and symptoms of Adrenal Fatigue Syndrome surface.

When couples fail to understand the cycles they go through, they often forget the positive elements in their relationship. Many relationship problems are the product of varying comfort zone settings. When one person hits one side of the comfort zone boundary and is already experiencing fusion anxiety, the other person might just be following his/her desirable depth of intimacy. As the first person reverses direction and comes back into the comfort zone, the partner might feel abandoned; their mutual anxiety explodes and accusations are thrown back and forth.

If we don't understand the role of anxiety in relationships, we're likely condemning ourselves to constant hurt. However, if we try to face our anxiety, we can alter the comfort zone boundaries and transform our relationship into a healthy, mutually reinforcing growth process. In such a relationship not only does our sense of self grow, but also the couple-bond tends to deepen.

In order to change a static comfort zone relationship into an actively growing relationship, we must train ourselves to stop in the middle of a conflict and engage in self awareness. We can ask questions like:

- How did this fight start?
- What am I anxious about?
- What about this situation feels so threatening?

Using these questions allows us to forge a path to self-knowledge and deeper peace in our relationships. Intimate relationships awaken our deepest anxieties, and therefore, if we use them intelligently, relationships have the capacity to help us grow as individuals.

When Removing Yourself Is Needed

The positive possibilities notwithstanding, it is also true that some relationships do not have the potential for growth, at least not without significant commitment to change. As we all know, we can't change other people, so one-sided commitment is not necessarily enough. In fact, being around a toxic person for a long time might greatly decrease self-worth, along with capability and competence. For this reason, you must stop the harm caused by another person (or more than one person); only then can you determine if a relationship can be maintained or must be ended.

First, recognize that if your life is distressing, only you can change the situation. Here are some tips on how to live a better life by nullifying the negative influence of toxic relationships:

- **Take Responsibility:** Understand that some part of you is contributing to the negative—toxic—behaviors. Then, ask yourself why you're willing to allow the behaviors to continue. What can you learn from your own behavior?

- **Set Boundaries:** Let your partner know that you won't be bullied or ignored. Describe what changes you want and tell your partner your expectations for the future.

- **Forgive:** Remember that individuals generally are not born toxic. Our environment and circumstances over time mold us into who we are.

Regain your sense of the good in the person beneath the surface toxicity.

Regardless of the ultimate outcome, learn to forgive and return love; we believe this is our primary purpose on earth. When possible, use love to heal one another.

- **List the positive characteristics of the person:** If you focus only on negative characteristics, the person will be negative whenever he/she is around you. By altering your focus, you influence the other person's behavior for the better.

- **See a new perspective from a neutral party:** Counselors, coaches, neighbors, or co-workers are individuals who likely have no bias for or against your relationship, whereas relatives and close friends may well have strong opinions one way or another. The key is to avoid creating a situation that triggers pity. You want another person to help you focus on the situation, examine the part you have played, and determine what you are willing to do to move forward.

- **End the relationship:** If nothing changes after you have tried all other constructive steps, you can walk away from your relationship with your head held high. You know you have tried to change the relationship but have also protected yourself from further harm.

Unless you transform or remove the negative toxic relationships from your life, you will generate the constant negative energy flow needed to sustain the toxicity. Clearly, this situation prevents healing Adrenal Fatigue Syndrome. The key to healing is first to recognize that the toxic negative energy must be transformed and rechanneled into the constructive energy needed to heal, and in the long run that will change your life for the better.

Key Points to Remember

- Relationships and well-being go hand in hand.
- Stressors come in all kinds. Emotional and mental stress tops the list, with toxic relationships being one of the most common contributors.
- Recognizing a toxic relationship is an important step to finding love and intimacy.
- In a toxic relationship, power struggles arise again and again, but no solutions are found.
- If a toxic relationship cannot be resolved, you must remove yourself by setting boundaries and taking responsibility for yourself. Terminate the relationship if needed.

Appendix A

Defining Our Terms

Throughout *Adrenal Fatigue Syndrome*, you will come upon certain terms and words that might or might not be familiar to you. Some terms come up in the text frequently, while others appear only once or twice. Rather than include a glossary at the end of the book, we decided to use this chapter to offer some easy, working definitions of commonly used terms. That way you can refresh your memory as they appear within the book. For example, throughout the text we refer to the components of the body's nervous system, and the definitions below will serve as a convenient reference. In other cases, we've defined terms we didn't define thoroughly when first seen in the text because they were used less often and we didn't want to stop the flow of information. Therefore, we added them to the list below. We also combined definitions of terms that logically fit together, rather than maintaining a strict glossary-style alphabetical order.

Acute/Chronic: When symptoms appear suddenly, we consider it an ***acute*** condition. For example, some common infections, such as colds, influenza, and pneumonia, come on quickly. The symptoms run their course and disappear as the body heals. Anaphylaxis shock is an acute allergic reaction to an allergen, and may be a life-threatening episode in an allergy considered to be ***chronic***, that is, an ongoing condition. Many conditions have both acute and chronic components.

Diabetes is a chronic condition with long term implications, but acute episodes of blood sugar/insulin dysregulation can bring on symptoms, such as fainting or severe weakness, serious enough to require emergency room visits. Rheumatoid arthritis and cardiovascular disease have both acute and chronic components. Avoiding acute episodes is one goal of managing chronic diseases.

Adaptogen: The ability to modulate and adjust to conditions as they change, whether or not these conditions are optimal. In the context of herbs, the term usually refers to the ability to bring the biochemical function back to normal, no matter if it is too high or too low.

Anabolic/Catabolic: Anabolic—The buildup phase of metabolism, in that our tissues are synthesized from the proteins and other substances we provide. ***Catabolic***—The breakdown phase of metabolism, in which the body supplies energy from the materials we have provided.

Autoimmune disorders: Many conditions, from rheumatoid arthritis to lupus to common allergies, result from the body's complex immune system. This system normally reacts to and works toward eradicating substances it perceives as "invaders." An autoimmune response occurs when the normal response is interrupted or disturbed and the immune system reacts to the body's tissues as invaders.

Challenge: Specific tests or protocols designed to prove or disprove a hypothesis.

Clearance: A measure of kidney and liver function. This refers to clearing a unit of a specific compound from a specific volume of plasma. The lower the clearance, the more compromised the function.

Crash: An abrupt state of reduced energy output and severe fatigue as the body reverts back to a simplistic form of function to conserve existing energy.

Decompensation: In medicine, when a previously working organ system or structure deteriorates, we call this decompensation. It can occur because of illness, stress, or aging. *Compensating* means the organ still tries to function despite the stressors. As Adrenal Fatigue Syndrome advances, the adrenals and other organ systems eventually begin to decompensate, potentially bringing on many confusing symptoms and organ system disorders.

Dysfunction: Impairment of a physiological function.

Dysregulation: Impairment of a physiological regulatory mechanism.

Metabolism: The overall term for the physical and chemical processes by which we produce, maintain, or breakdown the body's material substances.

Metabolites: The byproducts or results of metabolism. In addition, a metabolite is a product of metabolism that is more or less toxic to the organism producing it.

The nervous system: The central nervous system (CNS)—The portion of the nervous system that consists of the brain and spinal cord. The CNS gathers, stores, and controls information and is involved in all bodily and psychological functions, from breathing and walking to experiencing sadness and joy. ***The peripheral nervous system***—Consists of nerves and ganglia outside the CNS. It is divided into two parts: the somatic nervous system, which regulates musculoskeletal functions that help us deal with the outside world, and the ***autonomic nervous system (ANS)***, which regulates functions of the smooth muscles and glands within the body as described below.

Autonomic nervous system (ANS): The component of the nervous system that regulates involuntary actions, meaning we don't consciously control them, including heart and glandular activity. Multiple branches exist, the key ones being the **sympathetic nervous system (SNS)**, the **parasympathetic nervous system (PNS)**, and the **adrenomedullary hormonal system (AHS).**

Recovery cycle: When pertaining to Adrenal Fatigue Syndrome, recovery is the period immediately following a crash. Individuals will likely experience many cycles as they recover.

Stress: Put simply, stress is an individual's response to physical challenges, exertion, and events that create internal emotional pressure. We sometimes refer to the external events or circumstances as stressors, but our reactions are the source of stress, not the event itself.

Subclinical: Some conditions stay below the threshold at which we can detect and measure clinical signs and symptoms. For example, diabetes, hypertension, and hypothyroidism often produce symptoms, but clinical tests often show results in the normal range. We refer to this as a subclinical state. However, if left unattended, the condition can eventually worsen and abnormalities can appear on tests, hence, providing *clinical* evidence of their presence.

Unfortunately, subclinical states often occur but are ignored because the conditions are allowed to advance untreated until testing "proves" that the symptoms are real. In Adrenal Fatigue

Syndrome, current testing techniques may produce results that look like there is normal adrenal function all the way up to adrenal failure. Therefore, we don't recommend relying on lab results as the final answer in diagnosing complex medical conditions and, in particular, AFS.

We hope these definitions will help you get the most from this book. Now, we begin discussing other issues related to AFS, as well as the stages of Adrenal Fatigue Syndrome.

Appendix B

Finding the Right Practitioner

The right healthcare practitioner can change your life. In the case of Adrenal Fatigue Syndrome, this is usually the most critical piece of the puzzle. Why? Because the vast majority of those with AFS experience myriad convoluted symptoms that confuse all but the most astute clinicians trained in this condition. It's essential to know what each symptom means, along with its significance. As you can see from the case studies, the right professional guidance can mean the difference between successful recovery and persistent failure.

Due to the general lack of Adrenal Fatigue Syndrome expertise among conventional and even alternative health practitioners, finding the right practitioner is easier said than done. Those with advanced Adrenal Fatigue Syndrome face the greatest challenges, as many have already been abandoned by conventional medicine and left to self-navigate.

It's worth spending the time to find the right clinician. Generally speaking, he or she should be an open minded and nutritionally oriented health professional. Additional clinical experience in endocrinology, cardiology, psychiatry, and neurology is beneficial, along with knowledge of using natural compounds in a holistic setting.

Insist on someone who can individualize your care, and look for someone who can examine diagnostic tests but also see beyond them to discern how you feel. Seek the clinician who believes that managing your adrenals requires a comprehensive approach, including modifying your diet, lifestyle, and exercise; this person's approach to natural compounds is both gentle and systematic and non-stimulating. Remember that a wrong approach can worsen your condition over time. In today's managed care and specialized environment, this is not an easy task, but neither is it impossible.

The Doctor Interview

You are entitled to ask a doctor key questions before making an initial appointment, and then based on the answers, ask yourself if this person is receptive to new ideas. What is his or her philosophy on how stress can affect the body? This will give you clues as to whether this doctor is holistic or conventional.

Later, when you talk with this doctor, does he or she clearly communicate the reasons you feel the way you do? An experienced doctor will generally have little problem tying in your various symptoms and giving you a comprehensive explanation. You should be able to receive direct answers to your questions in a way you can understand. This is part of being patient-oriented.

You can also ask about the doctor's philosophy of the adrenal glands as a key to the body's overall well-being and your symptoms of fatigue, along with other organ systems associated with your complaints, during the investigation. These questions help you indirectly gauge not only the doctor's knowledge of the adrenal system, but the more subtle understanding of adrenal function and Adrenal Fatigue Syndrome.

How to Best Communicate With Your Doctor

A good relationship is a two-way street, so the more clearly you communicate your problems, the easier it is for the doctor to address the issues. Here are simple tips to facilitate good communication:

- Have confidence in yourself, but do not show either an overly aggressive or passive attitude.
- Keep a journal of your health-related events and symptoms, noting when they come on (time of day or relating to an event or the menstrual cycle, for example), how they affect you, how you feel, and how and when you recover.
- Write down questions ahead of your appointment, so you can ask good questions and make the most of your appointment time.
- Trust your instincts. Your body is always right. Persist in finding the care you deserve. Don't settle for less.

Although we realize many doctors do not welcome patient-generated research, and some even become annoyed when patients bring them information, we recommend that you help your doctor stay informed. Print out articles relevant to your condition that you believe may help your doctor understand your situation, and submit these to your doctor for perusal ahead of time. Our Adrenal Fatigue Center at *www.DrLam.com* contains numerous articles that we constantly update. You can direct your doctor to our website. Forward thinking doctors, the real visionaries, thank us for providing this information online so they can learn and better serve their patients.

You have also benefitted from this book and other articles. You can better explain and describe your symptoms when you know more about your body and various conditions. This in turn helps your doctor help you.

If your doctor does not understand or cannot explain to you what is happening with clear confidence, chances are you need to consider finding another healthcare professional.

Investigate Other Options

Here are several tips if you cannot find the right practitioner:

- Connect with others who've had similar symptoms and investigate what they did to overcome their dysfunction. Do be careful not to draw conclusions too quickly, however. What works for one person may not work for another. You may be able to find a doctor through those who have been helped.
- Use the Internet. Search Adrenal Fatigue Syndrome and study relevant sites. Focus on educational sites that offer scientifically based information. Our site *www.DrLam.com* is a public educational website that contains the most easily searchable complete library of material on Adrenal Fatigue Syndrome on the web. Many articles on Adrenal Fatigue Syndrome not present in this book are available online, along with the latest news, FAQs (frequently asked questions), and an archive of questions many have asked through the years. You'll also find video and audio presentations of lectures on Adrenal Fatigue Syndrome. Those who like to be kept up to date on the latest news on this topic can sign up for our free electronic newsletter.
- Be wary of Internet forums because views expressed are often skewed and not objective in nature. What works for one person can in fact be toxic for another. Be skeptical of anyone who purports to have simple, quick fix or break-through solutions. Watch out for those who post angry

messages or who are overly active online. These individuals may have hidden agendas or unresolved psychological or undisclosed physical issues well beyond AFS. Finally, be careful of one-size-fits-all approaches; these seldom work except for the mildest cases.

- If you are not sure whether you have Adrenal Fatigue Syndrome, or if you would like an assessment on the degree of your adrenal function, take our Three Minute Test in this book (Appendix F) or online at *www.DrLam.com.*
- If you have specific questions about your symptoms or condition, write to us directly from our website at *www.DrLam.com.* Each question is individually answered privately and in confidence.

Fortunately, travelling is not usually required in order to seek help. We serve clients all over the world. If you cannot find a practitioner with whom you are comfortable, or if you have no one to turn to, call us. (For details see our website.)

Our telephone-based nutritional coaching program is an individualized one-on-one program designed to facilitate the fastest possible recovery using natural measures. It incorporates many principles and techniques discussed in this book.

Appendix C

Glycemic Index Table

The glycemic index (GI) is a measure of how much blood sugar stress a food creates. Controlling blood sugar is one of the pillars in a successful anti-aging diet, and high blood sugar is a direct reflection of high sugar intake. Therefore, it's important to know what foods are low in sugar.

Below is a table of common foods and their glycemic index. To reduce blood sugar stress, concentrate on foods with an index at or below 70. This will help create a more even flow of glucose into the blood. If you are eating high glycemic index food like white bread, always try to pair it with a low glycemic index food. If foods are mixed, the resulting index will be between the high and low values.

Table 4, Glycemic Index Table, below lists common food products and their actual GI values. These numbers use glucose as a baseline, which is given a GI of 100. All the other values are relative to glucose.

Recommended: GI <70; Avoid: GI >70; If Diabetic or hypoglycemic: avoid GI >60

Legumes		Grains		Pastas		Bread Products	
Baked Beans, canned	68	Barley, pearled	25	Angel Hair	45	Bagel	72
Black Beans	30	Buckwheat (kasha)	54	Bean Threads	26	French Bread	96
Black Eyed Peas	42	Bulgar	47	Gnocchi	67	Kaiser Roll	73
Butter Beans	31	Couscous	65	Pastas, brown rice	92	Melba Toast	71
Chick Peas	33	Cornmeal	68	Pastas, refined	65	Pita Bread	58
Chick Peas, canned	42	Millet	71	Pastas, whole grain	45	Pumpernickel Bread	49
Fava Beans	80	Rice, brown	56	Star Pastina	38	Rye Bread	64
Kidney Beans	30	Rice, instant	85 –	Vermicelli	35	Rye Bread, whole	50
Kidney Beans, canned	52	Rice, white	70	**Snacks, Misc.**		Stuffing	75
Lentils, green	30	**Crackers**		Corn Chips	70	Tortilla, corn	70
Lentils, red	25	Graham Crackers	74	Fried Pork Rinds	OK	Waffles	76
Lima, baby, frozen	32	Rice Cakes	77	Olives	OK	White Bread	95
Pinto Beans	39	Rye Crispbread	67	Peanuts	10	Whole Wheat Bread	75

Legumes		Grains		Pastas		Bread Products	
Soy Beans	18	Stoned Wheat Thins	68	Peanut M&M's	32	**Fruits**	
Split Peas	32	Water Crackers	72	Popcorn	56	Apple	39
Dairy Products		**Cereals**		Potato Chips	55	Apple Juice	41
Ice Cream, regular	61	All Bran	43	Pretzels	82	Apricots, dried	35
Ice Cream, low-fat	50	Bran Chex	59	Rice Cakes	77	Bananas, ripe	60
Milk, regular	27	Cheerios	75	Rich Tea	56	Cantaloupe	65
Milk, skim	32	Corn Bran	75	Vanilla Wafers	77	Cherries	23
Yogurt, sugar	33	Corn Chex	83	**Vegetables**		Grapefruit	25
Yogurt, aspartame	14	Cornflakes	84	All Green Vegetables	0 - 30	Grapefruit Juice	49
		Cornflakes	84	All Green Vegetables	0 - 30	Grapefruit Juice	49
		Cream of Wheat	71	Bean Sprouts	<50	Grapes	46
		Grapenuts	68	Beets	64	Kiwi	52
		Life	66	Carrots	71 - 92	Mango	56
		Mueslix	60	Cauliflower	<50	Orange	42
		Nutri Grain	66	Corn	58	Orange Juice	51
		Oat Bran	55	Eggplant	<50	Papaya	58
		Oatmeal, regular	53	All onions	<50	Peach	35
		Oatmeal, quick	66	Parsnips	97	Pear	35

Legumes	Grains	Pastas	Bread Products
Puffed Wheat 74	Peppers <50	Pineapple 66	
	Puffed Rice 90	Potato, russet (baked) 90	Pineapple Juice 43
	Rice Chex 89	Potato, instant mashed 83	Plum 29
	Rice Krispies 82	Potato, fresh mashed 73	Raisins 64
	Shredded Wheat 69	Potato, new, boiled 57	Strawberries 32
	Special K 54	Potato, french fries 75	Watermelon 74
	Total 76	Radishes <50	
		Sauerkraut <50	
		Sweet Potato 54	
		Tomato 38	
		Water Chestnuts <50	
		Yams 51	
		Yellow Squash<50	

Adapted from D.J.A. Jenkins et al., American Journal of Clinical Nutrition, Volume 34, 1981.

For Glycemic Index of 1200 foods, here is the link: *http://www.mendosa.com/gilists.htm.*

Appendix D

Suggested Reading and Resources on the Adrenal Fatigue Syndrome

In addition to the books, CDs and DVDs listed in the front of *Adrenal Fatigue Syndrome*, here are additional free readings and resources from our website, *www.DrLam.com/afs/*. When on the site, just click on the topic of interest. Each will help you understand the scientific basis of our approach to Adrenal Fatigue Syndrome we take throughout this book.

- Acidosis
- Aging Brain
- Andropause
- Atrial Fibrillation
- Beef, Chicken, or Fish
- Blood Thinners and Nutritional Supplements
- Chelation
- Cholesterol
- Dehydration
- Detoxification
- DHEA
- Diabetes
- Eggs—Good for your body?
- Endometriosis
- Nutritional Supplements—To Take or Not?
- Omega 3 Fatty Acid
- Oral Health
- Progesterone
- The Big Fat Lie
- Estrogen Dominance
- Fibroids
- Heart Disease Prevention—A Complete Nutritional Approach
- Hypothyroidism
- Insulin and Aging:
- Magnesium and Aging
- Menopause
- Metabolic Syndrome
- Milk—The Perfect Food?
- My Doctor Is Killing Me
- New Markers of Cardiovascular Disease
- Nutritional Medicine
- Upper Limits Vitamin C and E Intake
- Water
- Where to Buy Supplements
- Why Conventional Medicine Rejects Adrenal Fatigue Syndrome

After Recovery

After your recovery from Adrenal Fatigue Syndrome, the natural progression is to embark on an anti-aging program where you begin to reverse the biological clock naturally, while keeping AFS at bay. We have a complete library on this in our website. The following articles are helpful and found also on *www.DrLam.com/afs/*.

Anti-aging Program	Dr. Lam's Smoothie Recipe
Anti-aging Strategies	Customized Exercise Routine
Blood Type Diet	Links to Various Health Centers
Osteoporosis	Calories That Count
Woman's Optimal Daily Allowance	Men's Optimal Daily Allowance

Links to Natural Protocols for Common Health Conditions

For the Avid Reader in Natural Health

You can download our free online ebooks from our home page at *www.DrLam.com:*

Beating Cancer with Natural Medicine
5 Proven Secrets to Longevity

Other Useful Links

New information and links on natural health and Adrenal Fatigue Syndrome are regularly added to our website library. These include many nonprofit educational organizations, links to scientific journals, periodicals, and additional recommended books.

Here is the link: *http://www.DrLam.com/links.asp*

Appendix E

3 Minute Adrenal Fatigue Syndrome Test

Here is a checklist of common symptoms associated with Adrenal Fatigue Syndrome. Check the boxes that are applicable. See your score below and find out what you can do about it.

- ❑ Tendency to gain weight especially at the waist and inability to lose it.
- ❑ High frequency of getting the flu and other respiratory diseases that tend to last longer than usual.
- ❑ Reduced sex drive.
- ❑ Lightheaded when rising from a supine position.
- ❑ Unable to remember things and unclear thinking.
- ❑ Lack of energy in the mornings and also in the afternoon between 3-5:00 PM.
- ❑ Feel better suddenly for a brief period after a meal.
- ❑ Need coffee or stimulants to get going in the morning.
- ❑ Crave for salty, fatty, and high protein food such as meat and cheese.

- ❑ Increased symptoms of PMS for women; periods are heavy and then stop, or almost stop on the 4th day, only to start to flow again on the 5th or 6th day.
- ❑ Pain in the upper back or neck for no apparent reasons.
- ❑ Easily startled.
- ❑ Decreased ability to handle stress and responsibilities.
- ❑ Body temperature is off balance; hands and feet feel cold, face feels warm, or hot flashes.
- ❑ Unexplained hair loss.
- ❑ Tendency to tremble when under pressure.
- ❑ Multiple allergies such as asthma, hay fever, skin rashes, eczema, hives, and food sensitivity.

Enter the number of checkmarks you have made: ______

What does your score mean?

If your score is 4 or below, chances are you do not have Adrenal Fatigue Syndrome unless your symptoms are quite severe. There may be other dysfunction in place. Adrenal Fatigue Syndrome is unlikely to be significantly involved, although we can't be sure without a detailed history. You can adopt many of the dietary and lifestyle recommendations in this book as they are generally conducive to good health. Group 1 and 2 nutritional supplementations (Chapters 20 and 21 in the book, *Adrenal*

Fatigue Syndrome) are generally well tolerated if your doctor approves. If you do not improve within a reasonable amount of time, write to us through our website with your score and what you did. We will give you our thoughts in confidence.

If your score is 5-9, you may or may not have Adrenal Fatigue Syndrome. Many conditions mimic AFS, so if you have not already done so, visit your doctor for further medical investigation. If you are given a clean bill of health but remain symptomatic, consider Adrenal Fatigue Syndrome. The higher your score on the test, the higher your risk of Adrenal Fatigue Syndrome. You also can adopt many of the dietary and lifestyle recommendations mentioned in this book, but be cautious when it comes to nutritional supplementation, as they can worsen the condition if not properly used. If you are not sure where you stand or what to do, then write directly and privately to us online through our website (*www.DrLam.com*) with your score and a brief history. We'll give you our assessment and suggestions in confidence.

If your score is 10 or above, it is imperative that you become fully educated about Adrenal Fatigue Syndrome and alert your doctor about this condition. The more severe your symptoms, the more dysfunctional your adrenal glands likely are. We *do not* recommend self-navigation as it often makes the condition worse over time. If you cannot find someone knowledgeable to help you, if you fail to improve on your recovery plan, and are not sure where you stand or what to do next, then write to us directly and privately through our website (*www.DrLam.com*). Let us know your score, a detailed medical history, and your main complaints. We will reply to you in confidence and give you some guidance.

This free test is also available online at our website *www.DrLam.com.*

Appendix F

Nutritional Supplement Blends for AFS

Not all supplements are created the same. Quality varies greatly, depending on ingredients and the manufacturing process. Inferior quality supplements can deter the recovery process and actually make things worse. Buying supplements based on price alone is a common recovery mistake.

To ensure the highest quality and consistency based on latest research, we have formulated our own line (Dr.Lam) of dietary supplements. They are made specifically for those with AFS and those who believe in using nutritionals to deter the aging process. Most people with AFS are highly sensitive. We have to be very careful about what we recommend. Knowing the exact blend and ingredients of each formulation gives us great insight and advantage on how to match each person's nutritional need with their body state during each step of their recovery. These products are made in the United States under strict manufacturing standards.

The complete line is available at *SupplementClinic.com*, the most complete online dietary supplement retailer dedicated to AFS, providing everything from supplements to books, video and saliva test kits. In addition to having reasonable price and excellent service, they ship worldwide. Royalties received go to support the ongoing mission of *DrLam.com.*

Some of the most popular of Dr. Lam's nutritional formulations designed for Adrenal Fatigue Syndrome are:

Quantamax®: Quantamax is a technologically advanced health drink formulated in a special matrix of mineral ascorbates, amino acids, co-factors, and immune-enhancing nutrients. This support provides the nutrients necessary to help rebuild and rejuvenate the important adrenal and cardiovascular collagen network in our bodies, leading to healthier adrenals, skin and decreased risk of cardiovascular disease. This blend formula provides for quick and gentle energy boosts without the over-stimulatory, spiky side-effect of ascorbic acid.

C-Support: C-Support is a cutting-edge blend of four different sources of Vitamin C including ascobyl palmitate, the fat soluable form. This formula provides a precise balanced ratio designed for sustained release to achieve optimal biological activity of Vitamin C in the body.

Pandrenal®: Pantethine, along with pantothenic Acid (Vitamin B5), forms a powerful blend in supporting adrenal glands and normal cholesterol levels in the body. Both are needed, and having the right ratio of each is important to harvest the synergistic effect. It is manufactured in a hermetically sealed soft-gel to deliver the purest and most potent combination possible.

Adreno-Blast™: The formula contains a blend of adrenal glandular, adaptogenic herbs, and four types of ascorbates designed to increase overall body energy, while decreasing exhaustion and fatigue. This is particularly useful for those in mild or recovering AFS when the body is stable.

LipoNano® C: LipoNano C represents a major breakthrough in the therapeutic nutrient delivery system of Vitamin C, with several key characteristics. First, Liposomal Encapsulation Technology (LET) is used. It combines nano-technology and bio-technology in a powerful way to take advantage of characteristics of liposomes similar to that made by Mother Nature, using natural ingredients such as essential fatty acids and phospholipids. Second, these liposomes are naturally strong and sized perfectly for maximum stability during transport and easy penetration at the cellular level, just as Mother Nature intended. Third, the liposomes contain nutrients and synergistic co-factors in a micro-bubble. Cellular bioavailability is significantly enhanced. Due to the high potency of this formula, always start a with small amount.

LipoNano® Glutathione: Glutathione, an antioxidant produced by the body that fastens to and gets rid of toxins, is necessary to help purge the body of poisonous metabolic waste and to maintain the immune system. When exposed to aging and stress, our glutathione levels drop. Synergistic co-factors, such as Vitamin E and B12, are important elements that enhance clinical outcome. Replenishment is critical to enhance AFS recovery.

About the Authors

Michael Lam, M.D., M.P.H., A.B.A.A.M., is a western trained physician specializing in nutritional and anti-aging medicine. Dr. Lam received his Bachelor of Science degree from Oregon State University, and his Doctor of Medicine degree from the Loma Linda University School of Medicine in California. He also holds a Master's degree in Public Health. He is board certified by the American Board of Anti-Aging Medicine where he has also served as a board examiner. Dr. Lam is a pioneer in using nontoxic, natural compounds to promote the healing of many age-related degenerative conditions. He utilizes optimum blends of nutritional supplementation that manipulate food, vitamins, natural hormones, herbs, enzymes, and minerals into specific protocols to rejuvenate cellular function.

Dr. Lam was first to coin the term, *ovarian-adrenal-thyroid (OAT)* hormone axis, and to describe its imbalances. He was first to scientifically tie in Adrenal Fatigue Syndrome (AFS) as part of the overall neuroendocrine stress response continuum of the body. He systematized the clinical significance and coined the various phases of Adrenal Exhaustion. He has written four books: *The Five Proven Secrets to Longevity, Beating Cancer with Natural Medicine, How to Stay Young and Live Longer, and Estrogen Dominance.*

In 2001, Dr. Lam established *www.DrLam.com* as a free, educational website on evidence-based alternative medicine for the public and for health professionals. It featured the world's most comprehensive library on AFS. Provided free as a public service, he has answered countless questions through the website on alternative health and AFS. His personal, telephone-based nutritional coaching services have enabled many around the world to regain control of their health using natural therapies.

Dorine Lam, R.D., M.S., M.P.H., is a registered dietitian and holistic clinical nutritionist specializing in Adrenal Fatigue Syndrome and natural hormonal balancing. She received her Bachelor of Science degree in Dietetics, holds a Master's Degree in Public Health in Nutrition, and a Master of Science degree in Nutrition from Loma Linda University, in Loma Linda, California. She is also a board-certified, Anti-Aging Health Practitioner by the American Academy of Anti-Aging Medicine. She coauthored with Michael Lam, M.D., the book *Estrogen Dominance* and numerous articles on Adrenal Fatigue Syndrome. Her personal research and writing focuses on the metabolic aspect of Adrenal Fatigue Syndrome.

She is married to Michael Lam and is an integral part of the telephone-based nutritional coaching team helping people overcome Adrenal Fatigue Syndrome.